Praise for Generation J

"... poignant, hilarious, and wholly genuine. [Schiffman's] unpretentious candor makes this book refreshing. Her style is engaging and articulate, and her deft interweaving of her own story with statistics, important Jewish writings, and anecdotes about the other Gen J-ers illuminates beyond the personal."

—*San Francisco Chronicle Book Review*

"A thoughtful, ironic, and piercingly insightful view on spirituality and Judaism from an informed and intelligent representative of Generation J ... an ultimately readable treat not only for the titular generation of Jews but for anyone who has ever examined a personal sense of spirituality and relationship with religion. Schiffman's quest to understand her identity as a Jew is both sincere and deeply spiritual. Yet, even in moments of profound spiritual awareness, Schiffman never takes herself too seriously, nor does she ever lose her ability to see the deeply ironic, humorous aspects of her journey. It helps, of course, that Schiffman is an immensely talented writer. Beyond her facility with words, however, Schiffman demonstrates a certain courage in gently but insistently probing issues of ritual and belief that will surely generate controversy in the very religion she seeks to embrace. To publicly question faith, even if the questioning is directed inward, is to leave oneself open to thorny criticism, for there is possibly no topic that engenders such emotional extremes as that of religion. The fact that Lisa Schiffman is able to pose these questions while underlining their universality makes *Generation J* a triumph." —*San Diego Union Tribune*

"Intelligent, curious, and engaged, Schiffman makes an appropriate poster child for Generation J. Her honest portrayal of her intellectual and spiritual journey across a wide swath of the complicated terrain of American Jewry mirrors her generation's search for meaning ... " —*Jewish Week*

"Seekers of the religious and spiritual, or those who are merely thoughtfully secular-minded, will find Schiffman's musings on her strenuous efforts to understand what it means to be Jewish in the 'post-Holocaust' age provocative, insightful, and funny." —*Booklist*

"[A] bold, unabashed, engaging narrative. . . ." —*Oakland Tribune*

"[Schiffman] has that charming, Anne Lamott–like ability to be spiritual and irreverent at the same time. This makes her a delightful guide into her own hand-wringing and soul-searching. Schiffman has created a mini-Talmud for her times." —*San Jose Mercury News*

"With a blessedly light touch, Schiffman, formerly an editor with the *San Francisco Review of Books* and until recently a nonobservant Jew, relates her beginner's quest for a Judaism she can genuinely practice and believe . . . [a] delightful spiritual narrative."
—*Kirkus Reviews*

"Well written and entertaining . . . Schiffman's chronicle presents a moving and gently told portrait of youthful American Judaism setting out on a brand-new wilderness journey." —*Los Angeles Times*

"An interesting sociological look at today's young Jews."
—*JUF News*, (Chicago)

"This is an important book about the condition of the American Jewish spirit. . . . This book must be read as a challenge as well as a harbinger of hope by all who care about the Jewish future in America." —Egon Mayer, Ph.D., director of the Jewish Outreach Institute and author of *Love and Tradition: Marriage Between Jews and Christians*

"Lisa Schiffman's *Generation J* is a remarkable account of self-discovery and self-analysis of what it means to be a young, secular Jew in a post-Zionist world. Diaspora Jewry has become more and more aware of the complexities and difficulties of being Jewish—not as a religious practice but as a cultural identity. Even the majority of Jews in Israel today are the mirror image of Lisa Schiffman—secular Jews who are conscious of their Jewish identity but do not see it as a necessary extension of any specific form of religious practice. Schiffman's voice is an important one." —Sander L. Gillman, University of Chicago, author of *Difference and Pathology*

"A wonderfully entertaining exploration of what it means to be a secular Jew in America today. Schiffman asks all the relevant questions conveniently ignored by more conventional authorities and dares to go where they fear to tread."
—Robert Eisenberg, author of *Boychiks in the Hood*

"Lisa Schiffman writes with the daring audacity of language and bold observations usually the private preserve of novelists. She's a born writer, and this is a terrific book."
—Kate Braverman, author of *Palm Latitudes* and *Small Craft Warnings*

"*Generation J* is the boldest book about the contemporary Jewish dilemma that I have yet to read. It explores and finally articulates the hidden contradictions between who we are and what we call ourselves. In doing so, it raises profound questions about not only the nature of Judaism in our world today but about the nature of faith, God, and worship for all."
—Lauren Slater, author of *Welcome to My Country* and *Prozac Diary*

gener

ation J

LISA SCHIFFMAN

HarperSanFrancisco
A Division of HarperCollins*Publishers*

For David,
who taught me the meaning of forever

and for my parents,
who taught me how to love.

In some cases, names and identifying details of people mentioned in this book have been changed.

The author thanks Joel Crohn, Ph.D., for permission to describe his "Ancestral Shadows" worksheet. Crohn, an ethnotherapist and practicing psychologist, is the author of *Mixed Matches* (Fawcett Books, 1995).

The author gratefully acknowledges the right to reprint "Poem Without an End" by Yehuda Amichai from *The Selected Poetry of Yehuda Amichai*, translated/edited by Chana Bloch and Stephen Mitchell. Copyright © 1996 by The Regents of the University of California. Reprinted by permission of University of California Press.

Bible quotations, unless otherwise noted, are from the Revised Standard Version of the Bible, copyright © 1946, 1952, 1971 by the Division of Christian Education of the National Council of Churches of Christ in the U.S.A. Used by permission.

HarperCollins books may be purchased for educational, business, or sales promotional use. For information please write: Special Markets Department, HarperCollins Publishers Inc., 10 East 53rd Street, New York, NY 10022.

HarperCollins Web Site: http://www.harpercollins.com
HarperCollins®, ☕®, and HarperSanFrancisco™ are trademarks of HarperCollins Publishers Inc.

FIRST HarperCollins PAPERBACK EDITION PUBLISHED IN 2000
Designed by Joseph Rutt

Library of Congress Cataloging-in-Publication Data
Generation J / Lisa Schiffman. —1st ed.
p. cm.
ISBN 0–06–251577–2 (cloth)
ISBN 0–06–251578–0 (pbk.)
1. Judaism—United States. 2. Schiffman, Lisa—Religion. 3. Jewish women—United States—Biography. 4. Jews—United States—Biography. I. Title.
BM205.S27 1999
296—dc21   99–20743

01 02 03 04 ❖/RRD 10 9 8 7 6 5 4 3

CONTENTS

ACKNOWLEDGMENTS IX

ONE   GENERATION J   1

TWO   THIS THING CALLED INTERMARRIAGE   14

THREE   THE ZEN OF BEING JEWISH   31

FOUR   KIKES AND QUEERS   47

FIVE   NOTES FROM THE FIELD   51

SIX   JUDAISM: THE BRAND   71

SEVEN   STRAY HAIRS AND PAINTED NAILS   77

EIGHT   THE SOUND OF GOD   94

NINE   THE KABBALISTS   114

TEN   KOSHER—ME?   123

ELEVEN   THE GLEANINGS   142

TWELVE   EXILE   161

ACKNOWLEDGMENTS

This book was lucky to have had two very supportive editors: Karen Levine and Caroline Pincus.

I thank Karen Levine for her insights, her kindness, and her understanding of the book's needs. My gratitude to Caroline Pincus for her ideas, her wisdom, and her warmth. Her two-year participation in the project helped make the book what it is today. To the other talented professionals at HarperSanFrancisco, who helped in many ways—my thanks.

I'm grateful to my agent, Joshua Greenhut of Witherspoon Associates, whose astute advice radically changed the book's direction; and I'm thankful to Kim Witherspoon.

Lauren Slater inspired me, gave me her ideas, and showed me how to write. Mark McCormick taught me what it means to believe, took the book's journey with me, and kept me gainfully employed. Dylan Schaffer offered original wisdom and lifted my confidence. Carolyn Grossman reviewed every chapter and asked for more. My husband, David Fore, who let me document part of his life, helped in ways too many to mention.

My parents, Murray and Malvina Schiffman, as always, sustained me with their love. My sister, Sandi Schiffman, cared and shared in my search long-distance. My families—both east coast and west—and my closest friends and colleagues graced me with their interest. For this I thank them.

Many people generously gave their time in interviews. My gratitude to all whose voices appeared in the book and those whose didn't: Norman Kleeblatt, Linda Steinberg, student rabbi Naomi Steinberg, Kaila Flexer, Andrew Tannenbaum.

Certain people entered at just the right moment: Jessica Lipnack, Peter Wiley, B. J. Bateman, Jeff and Rebecca Davis, Dave Cronin, Roslyn Roucher, and the staff of San Francisco's Jewish Community Library. Rabbi Jane Litman's help was invaluable. And lastly, author Kate Braverman taught me what I needed to know.

Generation J

I t was a Sunday just before the new millennium, which meant that somewhere, a workshop was going on. Somewhere, off the backroads of Boulder or at the outer edges of Manhattan, people were together in a small room, sitting cross-legged on the floor or straight-backed in folding chairs. They were doing things that would seem odd in any other setting. They were inhaling the scent of vanilla, for example, and writing down a memory. They were standing up in front of strangers and telling their most personal revelations. They were shedding their weekday wear of suits and ties, leaving behind their laptops and cell-phones. They were forking over personal checks in the hopes of finding out (in a cosmic sense) what it all meant. They were—once again, because the process never ended—trying to define the elusive boundaries that made up their identity.

I was no different. Early one Sunday morning, I wrapped my hands around a steaming cup of cappuccino and squeezed through a crowded Berkeley doorway into a workshop on Jewish identity. I did this voluntarily. I actually paid good money for a conference on Judaism and psychology.

In front of me, on small chairs with rigid backs, sat twenty psychotherapists, a lanky choreographer, and a few wispy graduate students. Most were women and all were hunched over their laps, writing furiously on a piece of paper divided into four areas—one for paternal grandparents, one for maternal grandparents, one for parents, and one for siblings. Each area contained the words: *I am a Jew, and to me that means* _____.

The workshop leader, ethnotherapist Joel Crohn, gave me a form as I entered. I was supposed to fill in the blanks by composing a line describing what being Jewish meant for each of my relatives. I took a seat and began chewing on the end of my pen. I usually despised psychological exercises. I either felt superior to them, a condition that I figured indicated some sort of delusions-of-grandeur neurosis, or I felt the absolute dread of hard work, as though someone had just asked me to mow a lawn with scissors. I eyed the door. Perhaps I could make my way out, bail before anyone noticed.

No. I hunkered down more deeply in my seat. I was there to find out more about myself, to make sense of the question that American Jews kept asking: What does it mean to be Jewish? Crohn strode across the room. "The name of this exercise is Ancestral Shadows," he said. "And by the end of it, you're going to hear many voices."

He closed the door. I was in it for the duration now. He pointed to a small woman named Deborah and asked her to choose people to play her ancestors. Role-playing. My palms began to sweat. I wanted no part. I averted my eyes, lowered my head. "You," she said, her voice in my ear, "maybe you could be my grandmother." When I stood up, she stepped back, assessed my face. "No, you look too nice," she said, waving her hand. "You can sit down."

Too nice? I thought of my never-leaves-New-York sister, who had once tried training me in nastiness. She said it was for my own good. In Manhattan parlance, *nice* meant *sucker*. It meant your new land-lord took one look at you, upped the monthly rent by a few hundred bucks, and kept the key-deposit money when you left. I narrowed my eyes at the small woman in front of me. She smiled, turned away, pointed to someone else in the group. I sat down, nicely, in my seat.

Soon her surrogate relatives began populating the center of the room. At Crohn's signal they stood in a cluster and began to recite their lines over and over. Imagine an entire family talking at once, saying different things. (If you're Jewish, this shouldn't be too hard.) They didn't listen to each other. They each said who they were as Jews, again and again. It was a dissonant, disorganized chorus, but in it I heard the shifting nature, the generational voices of Judaism:

SURROGATE GRANDPARENT 1: I'm a Jew, and to me that means following the rules without question.

SURROGATE GRANDPARENT 2: I'm a Russian Jew who escaped the Cossacks, and to me that means being Jewish is a hardship.

SURROGATE GRANDPARENT 3: I'm a Jew who fled Germany, and to me that means Jews are never safe.

SURROGATE GRANDPARENT 4: I'm a Jew, and to me that means making sure my kids are Jewish.

SURROGATE MOTHER: I'm a Jew, and to me that means feeling especially Jewish when my Catholic daughter-in-law comes to visit.

SURROGATE FATHER: I'm an atheist Jew—formerly a Communist—and to me that means religion is meaningless.

Crohn raised his hands to silence the buzz. "Now tell your ancestors who *you* are," he said to Deborah.

She paused. She looked at the group in front of her, skewed versions of her mother, her grandparents, her father. "I'm a Jew who's spiritual," she said, "and to me that means I haven't found my own way."

Wayfinding. That word came to me. An anthropologist, someone whose name I've long forgotten, once used that word to describe the process of mapping an identity. To him, identity was something always on the move, something difficult to track. It was strange terrain. To chart it properly you had to cover it on foot rather than peer down at it from a distance. To find your way, you had to cast yourself into the muck of life, explore, toss away the topographical maps.

My own Jewish identity was impossible to map. It defied the idea of precise boundaries, refused to have its coordinates pinned down and traced. Its borders shifted. There were variations and anomalies in the landscape. I knew this. Still, I imagined trying to map my own path. Was there a path for an ambivalent Jew? I wanted to create one.

In the crowded conference room, I looked at the papers on laps next to me, around me. People had begun to talk with each other. Everywhere, I heard lines of dialogue similar to those I'd written on my form. It occurred to me that most of us were third-generation American Jews. We had at least two grandparents who came, accent intact, from somewhere else. We had parents who had either followed a Judaism by rote or rejected the religion altogether. Our ages varied, but there we were, connected.

We were a generation of Jews who grew up with television, with Barbie, with rhinoplasty as a way of life. Assimilation wasn't something we strove for; it was the condition into which we were born. We could talk without using our hands. When we used the word *schlepp*, it sounded American. Being Jewish was an activity: *Today I'll be Jewish. Tomorrow I'll play tennis.* In secret, we sometimes wondered if being Jewish was even necessary. We could resist that part of ourselves, couldn't we? To us, anything was possible.

Crohn's voice interrupted my thoughts. Our time was up. Just before standing, I noticed a piece of chalk near my foot and bent over, grabbed it. As I walked outside to wait for the next workshop, I fingered it, turned it over in my hand. Keeping my fingers occupied was a compulsion. As a kid I kept twine, clips, or bits of soft metal in my pocket to tug, rub, or twist into shapes.

I grew up in Levittown, New York, where Jews were a minority. Someone's mother once asked me, in all seriousness, if Jews celebrated Thanksgiving. Someone's uncle once told me that Jews didn't exist. A young friend I'll call Toast once told me—as if it were some sort of consolation—that just before the end of the world, all Jews would turn into Christians. In junior high, while buying breakfast, I once heard a boy's voice behind me growl, "Is the Jew going to buy a Jew-bagel? Doesn't the Jew eat only Jew-foods?" He wouldn't let up. We almost came to blows.

If I could have ditched my religion, I would have. I was embarrassed to be a Jew. It made people notice me in a way that made me uncomfortable. I wanted to be like my friend Gina Gagliano. I wanted a house where Christmas lights hung outside all year, where the Virgin Mary was immortalized on dishware, where grace was something you and everyone around you at the dinner table said while holding hands.

Levittown was home to one of the largest crosses in the Western hemisphere. Wherever I was—outside the roller rink, at the deli, walking to the library—it loomed above me, a Christian skyscraper reminding me of what I was and what I wasn't. Levittown, where gold crosses graced the necks of my girlfriends, where boyfriends flexed their biceps so their tattooed crosses could dance. Levittown, where expressions like *Jew 'em down* and words like *kike* were heard as frequently as the roar of lawn mowers. Levittown, where people played bingo, burped as though it were a sport, slapped *Jesus Saves* on the bumpers of their cars.

Every other Friday, hundreds of kids left my public elementary school for a day of catechism class at a nearby church. On those days I sat in the back of an abandoned classroom and wrote stories, stared out the window, waited for my friends to return. With me were a handful of others: the emotionally disturbed kids, a few Jehovah's Witnesses, and three other Jews. I didn't go near them.

Once a group of Christian friends invited me to church. I remember a service of standing and sitting and standing and sitting. Being religious was exhausting. I remember Gina, the way she leaned toward me, saying, "Shhh—don't tell him you're Jewish," just before I knelt in front of the priest, said the words *body of Christ*, held out

5

my tongue as an offering. Smooth fingers placed a thin disk on my tongue. I stood up, felt the wafer attach like wet cardboard to the roof of my mouth. I walked to the back of the church, bowed my head against the back of a pew, waited for a Christlike feeling to arise in me. Nothing stirred.

"What's supposed to happen next?" I whispered, nudging Gina.

"Whaddya mean?" she said. "Nothing happens. We just go home."

Once I asked my parents why we never went to religious services. "I went as a kid and understood nothing," my father said. "Religions, all of them, are a hoax. They're a business. And religious leaders? They're the smartest businesspeople around."

My mother touched my cheek. "I don't go to synagogue. It's just not for me. The prayers, the sermons—they're not what makes me Jewish. I don't believe in them." She shrugged her shoulders.

What did it mean, then, to be Jewish? If the answer was found in ritual or prayer, then I wasn't a Jew. If the answer was in God—a presence in which I didn't believe—I'd never find it. What, then? I had no guide. I grew to ignore that part of me, the piece I didn't understand. Much later, when I began to wonder if something was missing from my life, I imagined what it would be like to be devout. I saw myself lighting candles on Friday nights, etching sacred words on my doorposts, being comforted by something greater than myself.

I did none of these things, though. I did instead what seemed logical: signed up for a class on documentary filmmaking. I wanted to film Jewish life rather than take part in it. I'd just gotten my degree in social anthropology. This meant that I was a trained outsider, a watcher; someone who knew how to question, film, take notes on other tribes. Now the tribe I planned to observe was my own.

I was living in Manhattan and wanted to film the Lubavitchers. With a classmate named Zoe Gold, a tall, stringy woman, I dragged a video camera and a bag of bulbs and metal poles (*lighting equipment*, said the film teacher) to Crown Heights. We never did figure out how to set up the lights, or even why we might need them. Instead, we stood on a corner, held out a microphone, and turned the camera on the scene before us.

It was village life, a shtetl. That first day, our lens caught sight of the accoutrements of devout Jewish life: images of flickering candles, fingers touching a mezuzah, the side panel of a Mitzvah Mobile, a poster of Rebbe Schneerson, a forearm wrapped in *tefillin*. Back at the editing studio, we realized that our first takes were an odd collection, a piecemeal presentation of Jewish Orthodoxy.

Zoe, behind thick glasses, looked up at me. "We need to talk to these people," she said, freezing a frame on the monitor. "We need to record their voices on tape."

As word got out in Crown Heights, people welcomed us. One family even invited us for Shabbat. The mother, who changed her wig twice during dinner, hadn't been born into Hasidism; she'd chosen it. At her table, we met people named Moishe and Jacob, Ruth and Shoshona. These people—who couldn't turn on lights after sundown, or carry money on Saturday, or drive to temple—seemed to have something that I didn't. They seemed whole. They knew who they were. However extreme, they inhabited their religion.

I asked Meyer, a Lubavitch teenager who looked vaguely Amish, why he had earlocks and wore dark suits and hats. "You want to know why we dress like this? I'll tell you. It's a reminder. We never want to forget, even for a moment, that we're Jews. And we want everyone to look at us and know it." He threw back his shoulders as he spoke, stared directly into the camera.

One day I went into Crown Heights without Zoe. I wanted to film what went on inside the synagogue on Eastern Parkway. This was the world headquarters for Lubavitchers, the place from which Rebbe Schneerson sometimes sent his words—via satellite—all the way to Russia. I went upstairs, the only place women were allowed. I sat behind the glass wall that separated us from the men below and filmed.

I saw the men, the way their bodies davened back and forth, pressed against each other. I saw hundreds of hands holding prayerbooks, rows of silken prayer shawls draped over bent shoulders. They chanted, these men, with their eyes half-closed. They moved faster and faster, back and forth. They were ecstatic. They could ignite the air.

Next to me, women wore wigs and heels, were lipsticked and powdered. A few nodded hello. I wondered why the women didn't daven. I wondered why glass was the material used to separate us from the men below, and why we had to be separated at all.

It felt like there was an invisible wall between me and the women surrounding me. There was a sheer wall made of glass in front of me. Around me were opaque walls bounding the synagogue, separating those inside from the unkosher world outside. *Walls*, I thought— *they separate Jews from the rest of the world and separate Jews from each other.* Suddenly, in the midst of so many other Jews, I felt alone.

I didn't belong. Not at this temple or at any other. Not, perhaps, anywhere in this religion. I had no one with whom to be Jewish. My friends were either not Jewish or too Jewish. My family was uncomfortable with organized religion—even their own. And me? I hadn't a clue about what it meant to be a Jew.

I was lost, a Jew without a path. I thought of Jewish history. For thousands of years, Jews had been wanderers, a people in constant migration. Because we'd been a people without a land of our own, because our physical geography was thus impossible to map, perhaps we'd tried instead to map our spirits. Jewish law, the ultimate religious map, explicitly mandates the right way to conduct yourself during nearly every stage, every moment of life.

If Christianity's message was *Follow your heart,* Judaism's was *Follow the directions.* Jews, however, never follow directions without asking why. They analyze words with the intensity of scientists. They find loopholes in the law, stretch the meaning of a sentence, spend hours turning over a single Hebraic syllable. They know that

Judaism is itself a language. And, like any language, it evolves, fits itself to different pockets of people, and is held up, always, by an undeniable structure.

In spite of our mandate to follow the directions, millions of Jews—the unaffiliated, secular, atheist, indifferent, or simply confused—are lost. We can't quite say whether our Jewishness is a religion, a race, or a tribal remnant. We don't keep kosher. We don't say blessings. We learn French, Spanish, Italian, but avoid Hebrew. We don't go to synagogue on Saturday but spend Sunday, at least in Northern California, at workshops to find out who we are as Jews.

It was time for the afternoon workshop. I'd signed up for one on Jewish healing and the body. The brochure had mentioned davening, dance, and something called a music ritual. I found the auditorium the workshop was to be held in and saw chairs arranged in a half-circle. Twenty people milled about, inexplicably avoiding the chairs. The workshop leader, a woman who could only be described in italics as *radiant*, stepped to the front of the room and introduced herself as Carol.

Ever since I'd watched the Crown Heights Lubavitch men in action, I'd been curious about davening. That was the first time I'd seen the body used as a religious instrument. Now I had questions. What kind of inner experience did the act of davening create? Was there a certain spirituality that could be accessed only physically? Could one daven alone, or was the energy of a group essential?

Carol asked us all to form a circle. "Hold hands," she said softly. "Now take deep breaths, exhaling to a count of three. One. Two. Three. Visualize your breath in different colors." While I mulled that one over, she asked us to step slowly to the left, then slowly to the right. The circle became an amoeba.

Carol turned on a tape player. There was a moment of static and then, unbelievably, Hildegard von Bingen's *Praise for the Virgin* filled the room. No one had expected this. Von Bingen was a twelfth-century scholar, mystic — and nun. Her ethereal sounds had made a comeback the previous year when they'd somehow fallen into the New Age slot at music stores. The man next to me dropped my hand. Yaakov was in his sixties and wore a skullcap.

"This isn't Jewish music," he shouted to Carol. "You want we should listen to this? We're Jews. This is Christological music."

Carol looked around at the rest of us to see if others were upset. No one raised an eyebrow. Like children, we continued to hold the hand of the person on either side of us. "It's spiritual music," she said, forcing a large smile. "Let's try moving in a circle again. C'mon now."

We tried. Yaakov took my hand again. But now the mood had changed. Feet seemed to be shuffling instead of stepping carefully. Carol sensed that a remedy was necessary and offered to change the tape. "Before we move on, does anyone want to bring up any other issues?" she asked.

Deborah, the woman from my morning workshop, stepped forward. "What about davening?" she said. "I'd really like to learn how to daven, how to pray using my entire body. That's what I thought this workshop would be about."

Carol's smile was now a bit strained. "Let's see if we can get to davening later," she said. She mentioned something about the sacredness of dance and began handing out an essay on erotic spirituality. "We're going to do a few more exercises," she said, "but first I want to find another tape."

As she bent over her tape collection and began rummaging through it, something extraordinary happened. Yaakov and the other Orthodox man in the group began to daven. A look passed between them and they simply nodded, then closed their eyes. They began rocking and created a rhythm in sync. They clapped their hands, somehow using their entire bodies to do so. They sang, and their voices came from deep inside their bellies. They made their own music, their own moment. People around the circle were mesmerized. It was hard not to stare. *Look inward to find what it means to be Jewish,* they seemed to be saying. Then Deborah also began to sway.

"Found it!" yelled Carol, oblivious. She slipped in a tape. The sound of old men wailing emerged from the speaker. The davening men came to a stop slowly, opened their eyes.

"Let's join hands in the circle once more," Carol said.

This was one circle too many. I disengaged and moved toward the back of the room, where I leaned against the wall with my hands in my pockets to watch the group. "Try to create your own physical vocabulary," shouted Carol. A man began to jump up and down, thrusting his hands high in the air.

My fingers touched the piece of chalk in my pocket. I pulled it out, knelt, and pressed its tip against the floor. Without thinking, I began to draw. I drew straight lines and then corners and curves. I drew half moons and small suns. When I tried to draw a star of David, the chalk suddenly failed me, slid over the waxy square of floor without leaving more than a trace. I convinced myself that this wasn't a sign. Then, while the group of adults in front of me flapped their arms, I rose and headed for the door.

Sometime after the Judaism and psychology conference had ended, I had a big think-through. What I realized is this: I'm not alone. I'm part of a generation of fragmented Jews. We're in a kind of limbo. We're suspended between young adulthood and middle age, between Judaism and atheism, between a desire to believe in religion and a personal history of skepticism. Call us a bunch of searchers. Call us post-Holocaust Jews. Call us Generation J.

Wayfinders, each of us. You'll see us everywhere: Jews in search of a perfect clarity. We're turning away from the religion into which we were born. We're turning to Wicca, to New Ageism, to Buddhism, to nothing. We're burning sage sticks at home and pounding drums in the forest. We're meeting with psychics, shrugging our shoulders at rabbis, listening to the music of twelfth-century nuns. Our chakras are opening, our kundalini is bursting. Our mouths open in the shape of questions. If we believe anything, it's that Allen Ginsberg may return as someone else. We light jasmine-scented candles and wait.

We've heard a few things. We've heard that Jews have caused the downfall of nations. They control everything. They make subversive movies about small extraterrestrials and realistic-looking dinosaurs. They've infiltrated the national government, rigged the social security system. They run Wall Street, the banking industry, and Zabar's. They own the garment center, the diamond district, and probably part of Chinatown. Who are they? Our grandparents. Our parents. And now us.

In America, we tell ourselves, it's possible to be too Jewish. We lighten our hair. We never use the words *kvetch* or *kvell* in public. Wearing a star of David around our necks is not an option. Vacationing in the Catskills would be unthinkable. Staying home on Friday nights seems absurd, not something to be taken seriously.

In our hearts, we know that we're missing something called Jewish pride. We're not unaware; we're just ambivalent. We have names like Marianne and Lauren, Ken and Doug, but we name our kids Zachary, Samuel, Elijah. We eat kasha varnishkes at home and pork fried rice outside. We drive German cars. We intermarry. We horrify Alan Dershowitz, Michael Lerner, and sometimes ourselves. We try to see in the darkness but are afraid there's nothing out there. We are, for better or worse, the future.

For now, we don't know what we believe. We tell ourselves if there is a God, we'd stop worrying. We imagine he'd leave messages on the wall—letters and shapes, things that look like upturned faces. We want a sign. There must be some sort of proof. Or perhaps there's a logic to it all, as with mathematical equations. We wonder if the constellations, the rhythm of tides, are reminders that God exists. We doubt it and push on.

Are we really Jewish? Yes. How do we know? Does it have to do with the measure of our skulls, with the slope of our noses, with the cryptic things recorded in German notebooks not too long ago? We're a community with a history of hatred leveled against us. Late at night sometimes when we're watching the news, we understand with certainty: it can happen again. It may start in Russia, in France, in Kentucky. Someone will lose a job, then a house, then a life. Nothing would surprise us.

For now we carry on, sipping cappuccino in the morning or sitting zazen, wondering where it is that faith begins. Someday we'll understand that we have all the knowledge we need within us. We'll recognize our kinship to certain old men in black hats and beards, to silken women slipping naked into mikvah waters, to young boys in skullcaps and earlocks. We'll know instinctively that a single molecule can carry the shadows of our ancestors.

One day, in the far corners of our minds, a thought will begin to grow. We can construct our own coordinates. We can build the pathways we need to this thing called Judaism. We can become fluent in the language of ourselves. I know this. In time, each of us will map the way.

THIS THING CALLED INTERMARRIAGE

1unch: Ben's Kosher Deli. David, my parents, and I. "Garlic-stuffed sausage, please," my husband—the last to order—said to the waiter. My father, mother, and I exchanged glances. David closed the menu and looked up, satisfied. Silence. We looked at David, stunned.

"What?" my mother finally asked. "What did you order?"

No one had ever, to my knowledge, ordered sausage at Ben's Deli. It wasn't a Jewish thing to do. You ordered lean corned beef on rye. You ordered pastrami with a side of slaw. You maybe ordered a long frank and split it with someone. You ordered a celery soda, no ice. My father, my mother, and I stared at David. If there'd been a comic-book bubble over our heads, it would have contained the words A SAUSAGE? My mother and I made eye contact again. All sausages were pork, weren't they? And wasn't this a kosher deli?

I pictured hand-signing David a frantic message: *We've all just been reminded that YOU'RE NOT JEWISH and we are.*

The Hawaiian waiter tapped his pencil tip against the table. He'd been waiting on booths at Ben's for about ten years and had perfected small gestures of impatience. "So that's it, right?" he said, looking us over.

"That'd be it," said David, nodding.

"Wait." My mother, puzzled, grabbed the waiter's shirtsleeve. "Is it a pork sausage?"

He looked down at my mother as she released her grip. He scowled. "Yeah. It's pork." He turned and walked away.

My mother's eyes widened. She looked at us. "Is that possible?" she said. She leaned over the table toward David. "What's in the sausage?"

David opened his mouth to answer.

"It can't be pork," my father said. He reached over, plucked a menu from between the pepper and salt shakers, and began scanning it.

David closed his mouth. He knew something was up.

"It's a kosher deli, isn't it?" my mother said loudly, to no one in particular.

"Maybe," said my father. He shrugged, closed the menu, furrowed his brow.

Perhaps none of us, I realized, knew exactly what the word *kosher* meant.

My mother and I stared at each other. This was unbelievable.

I looked for some sort of sign on the wall. Nothing. "Where's Ben?" I asked. "Let's ask him."

My mother pointed to a man flipping latkes at the grill behind the counter. Bits of burned shredded potato clung to his apron.

I jockeyed out of the booth and walked over. "Excuse me," I said.

Ben lifted his head. "Yeah?" He gripped the spatula like it was a weapon.

"I noticed you have sausages on the menu. Are they pork," I said, "or what?"

His face contorted. "*Pork?* This is a Jewish deli. A kosher deli. Pork? No. No pork. I can't believe this," he said loudly. A few people at the counter looked up, then turned back to their food. "Pork at my deli? No." He looked at me, his eyes slits. "Beef. Kosher beef. No pork." He lifted the spatula, waved me away like a fly.

Nearing the table, I felt victorious without knowing why. "Kosher beef," I yelled, squeezing back into the booth. My mother nodded in earnest. "I knew it," she said. It was all David could do not to roll his eyes.

I'll come right out with it: I've intermarried. If it sounds like a confession, it is. Because according to prevalent Jewish thought, according to Jewish sociologists and Jewish futurists and respected rabbis, I'm helping to cause the demise of the Jewish bloodline. Garlic all-beef kosher sausage notwithstanding, my husband and I are diluting and destroying the Jewish religion and race.

People say the American Jewish population is declining. Elliott Abrams writes about this tragedy at length in *Faith or Fear*. Alan Dershowitz, citing the same source material as Abrams, takes up the cause in *The Vanishing American Jews*. These men, like millions of other Jews, are in a panic. They say Jews, who used to make up about 4 percent of the American population, now constitute a mere 2 percent. Like an endangered species—bald eagles, desert tortoises— our existence is apparently threatened. The number of American Jews, says one report, may shrink to fewer than a million—perhaps as low as ten thousand—by the year 2076. And after that—poof!—we could eventually disappear.

The cause of this dwindling population? Jewish fingers point to intermarriage. Intermarriage! There's a plague. Too many Jews are marrying Christians, Unitarians, Buddhists, Hindus—anything but other Jews. Dershowitz and Abrams quote the National Jewish Population Survey of 1990, which reports that more than half of the weddings involving American Jews are now interfaith. And the vast majority of the children born of these unions are apparently not getting a Jewish education. Only 28 percent, according to one study, are being raised as Jews. The rest are in a religious netherworld.

Intermarriage! The word itself sounds like a directive from a technical manual *(place your pliers at the intermarriage of the wedge bolt and the pocket joint)* or a mathematical equation (✝ + ✿ = o). It sounds like almost anything but the union of two people in love.

Seven years ago, not too long before David and I were to swap rings, we talked about our ceremony. We saw it as a moment when we could define ourselves, acknowledge who we were, and think about who we might become. We would do this—declare ourselves and our love—and ask others to bear witness. The ceremony, I imagined, would be something David and I could create and nurture; it would start with a small seed of an idea that we'd water and tend during the six months or so before the wedding day.

I had grown up under the Christian calendar, Christian history, Christian laws. Christmas and Good Friday meant days off from school. Sundays, not Saturdays, were the holy days. Up until college, my schooling had come largely from a Christian perspective. My teachers had taught history, but the subject matter never seemed to contain anyone—other than Holocaust victims—who had any relationship to me. No one was ever Jewish.

Now, for the first time in memory, I wanted to acknowledge that I was Jewish. I didn't want to be married by a non-Jew. I wanted to be married by someone with the same heritage, the same bloodline, the same olive skin and prominent nose and outsider status as myself. There was more: I didn't want to give a Christian the authority, at this critical juncture, to change my life.

I realized, too, that I didn't want to be married by a stranger. I wanted a Jew who knew us—and had the legal power to marry. The list of the credentialed was short, to say the least. It contained one person. Jonathan. The husband of one of my closest college friends. David and I had flown to Los Angeles to attend his wedding just a year or two earlier. He was a Reform rabbi, just a few years out of rabbinical school.

I thought he'd do it. Didn't the Reform movement condone interfaith marriage? Wasn't he a young rabbi, not yet jaded or rigid in his practice? Wasn't he our friend? I pictured the three of us creating a ceremony that would respect each of our beliefs. I called him, asking if he'd marry us. I made it clear that I didn't expect a traditional Jewish wedding.

He said he needed time to think.

I waited four days before hearing from him again.

"No. Sorry," came through the telephone. Because David wasn't Jewish.

I felt precisely this: my religion had rejected me. It had rejected me and the man I loved. I got off the phone and told David.

"Well," I said, "we'll find someone else."

"Sure," said David.

We faced each other, embarrassed. In some sort of mute recognition of the moment, we embraced clumsily, then stepped apart. My religion had just rejected a man who wanted to live the rest of his life with a Jew, who'd shared the sweat and saliva and sweetness of a Jew. I was mad. No matter that I'd spent more than two decades rejecting Judaism. I wanted to be met with open arms.

"Fuck it," I said.

The search was on. A rabbi was out of the question now. "If even Jonathan won't marry us," I said to David, "why would any other rabbi?"

We asked friends for phone numbers; we cold-called and interviewed. A lineup of characters passed through our living room: the bearded Unitarian whose leisure suit reeked of Brut (for days afterwards the couch cushions exhaled the scent); the blithe woman from the Ethical Culture Society who *lowered* her ethical price to eight hundred bucks; the old warped justice of the peace whose raspy voice sank my heart; the pretty Universal Life minister friend of David's who—I found out one night—had slept with him before I came into the picture. These were our choices.

I had only an inkling then of what I know now: most rabbis won't marry an interfaith couple. The Jewish Outreach Institute recently surveyed more than three hundred rabbis nationwide and found that none of the Conservative or Orthodox rabbis would do the dirty deed. Slightly more than a third of the Reform rabbis said they'd officiate if the engaged couple promised—swore up and down—to raise their children as Jews.

Strings. There always seemed to be strings attached. I wondered, as I read about the survey, why marriage was so immediately linked, factory-like, to a production line, to output, to creating children. Was marriage merely about the continuation, the ensured evolution, of a race? What was the nature of marriage? Why did humans wed? What about love? Wasn't love what we all sought?

Bronislaw Malinowski, an anthropologist who reduced all social rituals and practices to matters of function, once referred to marriage simply as the licensing of parenthood. He and his colleagues—anthropologists who stumbled after tribes in the Trobriand Islands, in Borneo, in the southern Sudan—summed up the essence of marriage as the assignment of birthrights. Why were Jews acting more like a tribe than a religion? I was confused. We called ourselves a religion, but when push came to shove, our tribal instincts rose up. We were supposed to marry our own. We were supposed to keep our bloodline pure.

We were supposed to be endogamous. That word, which appears frequently in ethnographies, describes a rule saying that, by law or custom, you must marry your own. This, for better or worse, was the Jewish way. I thought of my grandmother. She had followed the rule to its extreme. She had married a Jewish man—her uncle. Her mother's brother.

Endogamy. In my grandmother's case, this rule turned out to be less than ideal. Her marriage lasted less than a year. She found herself pregnant and then gave birth to twins, my father and my aunt, as her husband was making his exit. Their marriage had been blessed by a rabbi. I'm not sure who divorced them, but I know my grandmother spent the next fifty years—the rest of her life—without a mate. For ten of those years her refrain to me was constant. "Get married," she'd say.

Eventually, I came across a rabbi who'd do the job. I met him at the outdoor wedding of our friends Christina and Jacob. "Here comes the Rainbow Rabbi," whispered my friend Mindy, who sat on the folding chair next to mine at the wedding. She turned to me and mouthed the words, "Oh boy."

I swiveled my head. I saw a man wending his way down the uneven aisles of chairs. His long gray hair flapped like a scarf in the wind. I was sure that his clothes, enveloping him like a fallen sheet, were made of hemp. I watched as he raised a wooden panpipe to his lips and blew. "I don't believe this," hissed Mindy to me. "I know what Christina told him: no singing, and *no* instruments."

I knew without looking that his shoes were open-toed. I knew that he lived somewhere far out in wooded Marin County, playing panpipe tunes from his redwood deck and dipping naked into afternoon hot tubs. I knew, from Jacob, that his price was a cool seven hundred. He met with you twice: once to get your vitals, and once to pronounce you, before God and the state of California, husband and wife.

I don't remember the rest of the wedding. Just one moment stands out: the Rainbow Rabbi stood before Christina and Jacob, facing them and a hundred onlookers. He smiled. He leaned back his head, opened his mouth, and let out a howl. It took minutes before I realized that he was singing. I caught David's eye. I shook my head. No. This was not what our wedding would be like. No way.

We decided to take a break from our search. The minute we did, my mother went into action in New York, where David and I were to be married. Every day I'd come home from work in San Francisco, head to the phone, and listen to my mother's message. "What about a Unitarian who used to be Jewish? I just heard about a man in North Bellmore. I'll find his number for you, sweetie."

Months passed. The Unitarian Jew didn't work out. My mother managed to corner the mayor of Glen Cove, who said he'd marry us, only to back out when he realized that we didn't live in his town.

With only two months left until the wedding, we flew to New York to meet with the caterer and the crew at the Harrison House, an old mansion that would house the shindig. Barry, the wedding planner, called us into his office, an overstuffed room about which the word *floral* would be an understatement.

My mother immediately told Barry our predicament. He looked at me in shock. "You haven't booked anyone to marry you yet?"

"No, I—"

He grabbed a piece of paper from his notepad and penned a phone number and name on it. "Call him," he said, handing me the paper. "You won't regret it. He's fabulous. He's a cantor and an opera teacher. And," he paused before the finale, "he played the rabbi in *Goodbye, Columbus*."

My mother threw up her hands. "Fantastic!" she shouted. She looked at David and me. "He played the rabbi in *Goodbye, Columbus*," she repeated. "Honey, you've seen the movie, haven't you? No? So you'll rent it before the wedding."

David was smiling. He looked at me, gave me a sly thumbs-up. The whole thing appealed to his sense of the absurd, I could tell. We'd be married by someone who'd played a rabbi in a movie. It didn't matter that we'd never seen the movie, that we probably never would see the movie. This rabbi would be even better than the real thing. I looked at Barry. "Thanks," I said. "You've saved us."

Two nights later, we drove to the house of Mr. Benedict. He was tall and distinguished, with the posture of an actor. He didn't wear bad cologne. He wasn't part of a religion oxymoronically called Ethical Culture. He hadn't slept with my husband before I came into the picture. He was therefore, in my mind, perfect.

He told us he'd married five thousand couples.

"At once?" piped David.

Smiling, he said, "No, two by two. And what could be better than marrying two people in love?" He walked us around his living room, where wedding photos of entwined couples, at least a hundred of them, smiled from behind the grand piano, above the mantel, along the walls. They wrapped around corners and up the staircase. He brought us back to the couch and motioned for us to sit down.

"Anything at all that you'd like me to read aloud during the ceremony?" he asked.

David put his hand inside his jacket pockets, fumbled for something. "I have a quote I'd like you to read," he said.

"You do?" I was surprised. He hadn't mentioned this before.

"Of course," he said. "It's a Nabokov quote."

David patted down his chest. Nothing. He stood up, thrust his hands into the pockets of his pants. Nothing. He pulled a hand out and a little yellow stickie floated to the floor. "Found it!" he said. He scooped up the stickie and put it on the coffee table. Then he stroked the back of my neck lightly and read aloud a single line: "Love with all one's heart, and leave the rest to fate."

Six years later. I was in my cramped home office in Oakland. David, a writer and software designer, was at work in Palo Alto. He'd just emailed me a small article, a not-so-subtle message about the joys of parenthood. Below my computer screen, on the desk in front of me, was a *Jewish Week* article I'd pulled off the Web. The headline, in thick black letters, shouted, **New York Rabbi Blesses Lesbian Union of Assistant Rabbi.**

According to the article, Reform rabbi Jerome Davidson had blessed the union of his assistant rabbi and her Jewish lesbian lover at an *aufrauf*, a prenuptial celebration. The act had infuriated many in his congregation and had incited heated discussions. Why? One of his congregants had put it succinctly: "It doesn't make sense. How can he sanction homosexuality—something the Torah forbids—but refuse to perform an interfaith marriage?" Just below the surface was the sentiment *How can he marry queers but not my own kid?*

According to the article, Rabbi Davidson had been grappling with the rabbinical issues surrounding marriage for years and was now willing to bless more than just the aufrauf for gay and lesbian Jewish couples. He was open to performing the wedding ceremony itself. And—perhaps even more surprising—he was reconsidering his stance against intermarriage.

I wanted to know more. I called Rabbi Davidson at his congregation in Great Neck. I put on my anthropologist hat: I hadn't gone through the grueling rite of getting a master's in social anthropology for nothing. It had been ten years, but still I knew the ropes. I'd be objective, dispassionate during the interview. Or so I thought. As it turned out, I discovered something about myself before the end of the conversation.

On the phone, we introduced ourselves. It turned out that his synagogue was near Ben's Deli, scene of the momentous garlic-stuffed sausage incident. I decided against telling that story as an icebreaker. Instead, I kept my opening short. I said I was Jewish—a secular Jew—and my husband was a lapsed Unitarian. I told him we'd been turned away by a rabbi when we were about to get married. Then I asked him to talk about his stance on marriage.

He dove right in. "The issue of same-sex marriage is about two Jews who want to have a Jewish home," he said. "They want to share their life together permanently and may want to have children. They want the blessing of their religion. And I feel that in the most meaningful interpretation of Judaism, that's something I should do." His voice was deep, thoughtful. I liked and trusted him immediately. He spoke with conviction, with passion.

He paused, then continued. "Interreligious marriages are another subject. For a long time—even before this issue with the same-sex marriages, and after it as well—I've been struggling with what a rabbi's role should be in such a marriage. I've asked myself, *To what degree, if at all, should a rabbi become involved?*"

I was holding my breath. With surprise, I realized what I wanted him to say: every Jew should have the opportunity to be married by a rabbi. It's a birthright.

He said instead, "I've reached the point where I'd perform an interreligious marriage for certain couples. But the non-Jew can't have a connection to any other religion. He or she has to commit to a relationship involving a Jewish home and Jewish children. The non-Jew has to study Judaism, affiliate with a synagogue, and commit to a Jewish life. Such a couple, I could marry."

He wouldn't have married David and me. No big deal, I thought. My hands were suddenly cold. I became aware of my wedding band, which felt loose. I pulled it off my finger and put it on the desk.

Rabbi Davidson continued. "Today I would say to people like you and your husband, Look, if you're willing to commit to a Jewish home and the Jewish faith, then I think your religion should bless your marriage. The question would be this: Can your husband embrace a Jewish life? Will he set a seder table, stand next to you when you light Shabbat candles, bring his child to religious school, share in the life of the Jewish community?"

I had never myself set a seder table, nor had I lit Shabbat candles. What, exactly, was a Jewish household? Had I grown up in one? Was it a matter of ritual and education? Was my home with David—our tiny apartment—a Jewish one? I doubted it. Not by Rabbi Davidson's standards. Was there a place in Judaism for my marriage? Apparently not.

"How do you define a Jewish home?" I asked.

"A Jewish home? It's one where there's a ceremonial and ideological expression of Judaism. Celebrating Shabbat and the Jewish holidays, Hanukkah and Passover—these are important. And Jewish values are important: tolerance, understanding, acceptance, and peace. These values are expressions of Judaism."

Tolerance and understanding. If these were Jewish values, why didn't Judaism encourage me to be tolerant of David as a Unitarian? Why did I have to override his religion in our home? Acceptance. If this was a Jewish value, why did so many Jews—members of Rabbi Davidson's congregation even—oppose gay and lesbian marriage? I didn't raise these questions out loud, though. Now wasn't the time for a debate.

Rabbi Davidson was still speaking, but I was distracted. I swiveled around in my chair, scanned my bulletin board. There was a poem from *Davka* magazine called "Jesus the Ex-Jew," by someone named Sparrow. Next to it were photos. I leaned forward, peered at a strip of dime-store shots of David and me. Four black-and-white frames, with our pose in each one goofier than the last. We'd stuck out our tongues, bared our teeth, licked at the lobe of each other's ear.

Rabbi Davidson became suddenly quiet. Then he said softly, "It's always very painful to turn away someone that you want to help because your principles don't allow you to do it."

I felt a pang in my chest. I'd been waiting for this voice, coming from a man I'd never met, to bless me, to say that my life was a valid expression of Judaism. Why? What could I gain? It didn't make sense. Yet I wanted Rabbi Davidson to bless me, bless my marriage. I wanted in. I wanted him to say that he would marry a Jew to a non-Jew, even if neither one was religious. Rabbi Davidson had known this before I did. He'd known that our phone call was more than a matter of anthropology, of bland inquisitiveness. He'd known that he couldn't offer the gift I sought. Yet still he'd agreed to speak with me.

We were Jews at an impasse, connected by the tensions of interpreting a heritage. I shifted in my seat. I steered the conversation elsewhere. I still wanted answers. "Does Jewish tradition prohibit interreligious marriage?"

"Yes," he said. "According to Jewish tradition as reflected in *halakah*, Jewish law, it would clearly be ruled out. A Jewish marriage requires two Jews, two heterosexual Jews who are going to have a Jewish home and family."

Did he say a Jewish marriage required *heterosexual* Jews? I made a mental note to follow that up.

"The Torah, however, is less clear about the issue. The Bible itself has many, many, many examples of intermarriage. Moses intermarried. Joseph intermarried. But their spouses became part of a Jewish household. And their children were considered Jews." He paused. Then he said, "Maybe we're working our way back to a more biblical experience right now."

Maybe we were. There seemed to be so many ways to live a life according to the Bible. It was all a matter of interpretation. The rules of Judaism, I realized, were full of loopholes.

I asked Rabbi Davidson to backtrack for a minute. "You said the Torah calls for two heterosexual Jews in a marriage. Yet you choose to interpret the Torah in a way that allows you to accept gay and lesbian marriages. Why don't you interpret the Torah in a way that permits interfaith marriage?"

I felt like an ill-prepared attorney trying to lead a witness.

The rabbi exhaled, then got tangled in his words. "You see, Judaism, the Torah—look." He stopped to gather his thoughts, then began again. "It says in the Torah that a man may not lie with another man as with a woman. It's considered an abomination. But the Torah understood homosexuality as a homosexual act on the part of two heterosexuals. Often, when it took place back then, it was thought of as a cultic expression. Or it happened in a time of war, or it represented some kind of oppressive, coercive situation.

"The Torah couldn't forbid what it didn't understand. Today we know that homosexuality is an orientation. It's not a perversion of a heterosexual activity. It's not a choice. It's the way people are. Therefore, if a Jewish lesbian wants to marry another Jewish woman, if they want a permanent, committed relationship, there's no reason why they shouldn't be blessed by Judaism.

"Think about it this way," he said. "Judaism isn't a static faith. It's an evolving, developing religion. Sometimes by revolution, sometimes by evolution, but change is really as integral to Judaism as any other aspect of our faith."

We ended our conversation there, because Rabbi Davidson had run out of time. We said our goodbyes with care and hung up the phone. I thought about cultural change. Mary Douglas, an anthropologist, had once written about something she called a thought style. She said that any society developed its own thought style—an agreed-upon set of principles about how the world is, about what's dangerous, about what's acceptable.

A thought style, once established, is difficult to change. Jews, by and large, believe that intermarriage is unacceptable. It's dangerous, to Alan Dershowitz. It's forbidden by law, to Rabbi Davidson. Never had I heard anyone propose that a marriage like mine, an interfaith union, could benefit the Jewish people.

What would it take to change this belief, to alter a thought style so pervasive that no one had challenged its veracity? Rabbi Davidson had said that Judaism was still evolving, that it had always evolved, either by evolution or by revolution. My vote was for revolution: a revolution in thought. I looked down at my wedding ring, which was still on the desk. As I slipped it back on my finger, I wondered how that revolution could begin.

My cousin wore a hot-pink minidress to my wedding. My father seemed to emanate a kind of light all day. My friend Mindy was there, breezing through clusters of guests, leaving the scent of Chanel No. 5 in her wake. The champagne was poured early on. I had my first glass in the morning, when my mother discovered that she'd worn shoes the wrong shade of gray and announced that she was driving back home to change.

"Mom," I said, trying to hold back a wave of panic. "You're not going anywhere. The ceremony begins in fifteen minutes."

Guests, a hundred of them, had already seated themselves on the chairs outside. From my perch on the upstairs terrace I looked out at the expanse of lawn, at the round lattice tabletops and their white umbrellas, at the women in their summer hats, and thought of *The Great Gatsby*. Small dramas were occurring everywhere. One of my relatives, mistaking one of David's friends—a Chinese physicist—for a waiter, asked him for a Coke without ice. The musicians were late. Our rings were misplaced and then found. Barry was everywhere at once, a choreographer and set designer. He tore through the garden, stopping in front of David with a gasp.

"You absolutely must wear a handkerchief in your suit pocket," he said. With a flourish he snapped out his own and transferred it expertly to David's jacket, where one white corner peeked neatly out of the pocket.

Then it was showtime.

We stood in front of Mr. Benedict. He said the things that were important. Talk enough and listen enough, he said. Follow the rhythm of each other's silences. In a world that reels, hold onto each other. Be impossibly kind. Open yourselves to pleasure, he told us, as well as to pain, because you will share both.

Then he directed us to lift our eyes, to look at each other. Notice the moment, I thought. I tried to memorize David's face, the way his blue eyes changed with the light, the way his lips, moist, were parted.

Mr. Benedict looked at us when he recited Nabokov: "Love with all one's heart, and leave the rest to fate." He was about to say something else, but David wasn't waiting for the next pronouncement. He wrapped his arms around me, lowered me into a dip, and kissed me. Mr. Benedict, sensing a lost moment, declared us husband and wife. Then he burst into an aria. That was it: we were hitched.

Afterwards, we were swarmed by a loving crowd of well-wishers. Our friend Jonathan, the rabbi who wouldn't marry us, made his way to my side. He hugged me. "Congratulations," he said. "It was a beautiful ceremony."

As I hugged him back, I fought down my thoughts. *Do you, somewhere, deep down, disapprove of my marriage? Do you think it any less than yours?*

"Thanks," I said, as we broke the embrace. He was my friend. I felt a wave of sadness. There was nothing else to say.

• • •

Not long ago, when David and I were visiting my parents on Long Island, I found a book in their public library's Judaica section. It was about the Talmud. I sat cross-legged on the floor in front of the stacks and began reading. It was there, surrounded by shelves holding thousands of pages on Jewish spirituality, on the vagaries of God's will, on the meaning of Jewish migration, that I discovered that the Talmud had never been completed.

The author said that the Talmud had never been declared finished. No one had ever made an official or public declaration that the work had reached its end. The Bible, by comparison, had eventually been completed after many stages of compilation, and it was made clear that nothing more could be added. Not so with the Talmud. The author proposed that the Talmud holds out a constant challenge to continue the work of creating Judaism.

The next day I visited Rabbi Davidson. He took my coat, shook my hand warmly, motioned for me to sit down.

I sank into the chair that faced his desk. "The Talmud," I said. "It was never really finished, was it?"

He looked at me, puzzled. "When you say *finished*, what, exactly, do you mean?"

Finished. I meant finished. No one had told me this before. The Talmud is waiting. Jews can spread open its pages, bend back its spine, ink a note in the margins. We are, always have been, people of the book, lovers of words. We abide by words because they mark the world, they make us holy. In the end, they're what we use to define ourselves.

The Talmud. It was there in the rabbi's office somewhere. I knew that it wasn't the work of one person but had been compiled by many scholars over a long period. They argued, edited, gathered bits of wisdom. They believed that no subject was too strange or remote to be studied. They looked at life closely, examined its problems, debated solutions.

In the book I'd read at the library, the author said that the Talmud was, in large part, a work framed by questions and answers. Even when questions weren't explicitly stated, they formed the background. It occurred to me there, in the rabbi's office, that it was time for us—for Jews—to recast our questions.

That night in bed, I looked down at David sleeping next to me. His leg was thrown casually over my own. His hand, shades lighter than my olive skin, rested on my stomach. I ran my fingers through his blond hair and he stirred slightly without waking. I looked at his face closely, as I often do when he sleeps. Fine lines had begun to etch themselves lightly at the corners of his eyes. I found them beautiful.

We were a hybrid couple, like hundreds of thousands of interfaith couples. We were an expression of love. We were an expression of Judaism. We had to be, because I'm Jewish. We, and others like us, were part of a Judaism that no one had yet named.

The Talmud was waiting. It would bare its pages for our pens, allow our fingers to trace invisible messages. Nothing, after all, was too strange or remote to be studied. Life was everywhere. The Talmud knew this. It was waiting for us to recast our questions. It was waiting for us to continue to write ourselves, and in so doing, to invent the future. This would be the revolution.

CHAPTER 3

THE ZEN OF BEING JEWISH

On my way to the Buddhist monastery, my allergies struck. Sneezes, coming out like machine-gun fire, doubled me over. My head felt like a wet washcloth. My eyes were red wounds. The time was 6 A.M. and my body hadn't yet fully awakened. I watched my feet land clumsily on the pavement. Thwack. Trip. Thwack. Why had I promised to take part in early-morning zazen?

At the monastery gate I reached for the latch. Damn. I wasn't tall enough. With horror, I realized I'd have to bang on the gate until someone heard. For the next several minutes, the morning had no sound other than my fist striking wood. I was certain each bang irritated the monks who were inside, calmly contemplating the experience of being alive. Through the crack, I saw a shaved head coming toward me and recognized Pam, the Buddhist novitiate who'd invited me to the service. She smiled, pretending I hadn't just committed an act worthy of negative karma.

At the doorway of the temple we took off our shoes. As Pam described her daily practice, my nose began to run. I excused myself, blew with the necessary gusto, and told her I was scared I'd sniff during meditation. She frowned, a look of disapproval flitting briefly across her face. She recovered quickly, readjusting her expression to one I interpreted as full acceptance.

"Each person has a different zazen experience," she said. "Some people sit silent and almost motionless the whole time. Others make the small sounds they need to and adjust their body position. Whatever you have to do in the beginning is fine."

My breathing got better and better during meditation. I was surprised at how much I enjoyed the act of sitting, letting my sight get foggy, and counting breaths back from ten to one. I managed to empty my mind several times, for long stretches, until the abbot interrupted. He'd just returned from Japan, he told everyone in the small temple.

"You alive," he said from his *zafu*, the meditation cushion behind me. "Zazen makes you know you alive." He went on and on. His wooden voice jarred me. My mind forgot to count breaths and instead wandered. It traveled back to my time in Taipei. I remembered my landlady there, who'd befriended me. While I'd folded *jiaozi* skins in her tiny kitchen, she'd wokked greens in hot oil, talked over her shoulder at me in Mandarin, told me stories about the Japanese occupation of the island.

After the abbot finished, I found I couldn't get back into a meditative state. I felt foolish perched on a pillow, staring at a cedar wall. Wasn't I Jewish? Why was I there? My right leg, twisted into a half-lotus, was beginning to cramp. I wondered, not for the first time, what I was trying to find.

My flirtation with the East began nearly fifteen years ago. I was an avid, if not obsessive, student of Chinese. I traced characters on my palms, papered my walls with tips on phonetics, spent hours on end making sounds that none of my college roommates understood. The language, with its mysterious symbols and musical intonations, fascinated me. The culture captured me. During college I spent summers in Shanghai—eight-hour days with teachers in Mao suits—then a year in Taiwan.

Once, when I was on autumn break from a difficult semester, my college boyfriend, a beautiful man, convinced me to meet his family. His father was a well-known rabbi of a large congregation. After his family sat down to dinner, the rabbi turned to me. "So," he said, "I understand you have a great interest in the East." He raised his fork, waved it toward me. "But what about your own religion?" I realized, with surprise, that he was angry. "You study Chinese? You've lived in China? But you don't study Hebrew? You've never been to Israel? This I can't understand." And with that, he turned his attention to his plate of food.

What? Why would I study anything Jewish? I clenched my napkin and said nothing. For years afterwards, long past the breakup with my boyfriend, his father's words rose up to meet me.

For a long time now, I've wanted the internal peace of a Buddhist monk. I've wanted my days to pass by in moments of Zen. Once, for a period of about two hours, I was totally committed to the idea of practicing Zen cooking.

"Babe, sit down," I said to David, grabbing him as he walked in the door. I needed his full attention. "From now on, I'm going to cook every day. I think we both should. We go out to eat too much. We're missing something essential. We need to start with our own ingredients, fresh, then do the chopping and salting, wrapping and peeling. You with me?"

My husband is a man of wisdom. He knew better than to mention that I cook dinner once a month. Or that cooking, to me, means buying tomato sauce and heating it up at home. He stared at me.

"Look," I said. "I just finished reading an interview with Bernard Glassman. The guy's a Zen master. He talks about cooking as a spiritual practice. He says that when we cook with Zen attention, we learn to live life more fully in each moment. He says that with awareness, even an ordinary act, like paring an apple, is transformed."

I said a lot more. I went on and on. I made lots of promises and got irritated at David for not jumping on the bandwagon. He wouldn't commit to practicing Zen cooking, whereas I was about to change my entire being. He just said he'd do what he could. I cooked fish that night, and it was lovely. The word *Shabbat* flashed through my mind. Perhaps living with full attention to the moment is what happens every Friday night at sundown in religious Jewish homes. Perhaps Shabbat was a kind of Zen. And Glassman, I realized suddenly, was a Jew.

The next morning I awoke in a funk. I grabbed the granola jar, opened it, poured the stuff into a bowl, and ate. I'll do the Zen thing at lunch, I thought. David, who got up after me, measured a half-cup of Irish oatmeal into a pot and cooked it with milk, nutmeg, and vanilla. He sliced delicate pieces of apple into his bowl, ate slowly, kissed me, then went off to work.

I crept to the computer and worked at home until lunchtime. Hunger struck. I looked in the fridge. The bag of limp lettuce and scallions and the package of smoked tofu depressed me. Yet buying a sandwich seemed very un-Buddhist. I went back to the computer. Hours later, when David came home from work, I was famished. "Indian?" I suggested.

He opened his mouth to say something and then closed it again. We ended up at an Indian place in downtown Oakland. The next night it was David who cooked dinner again—a curried rice dish with currants. Sometime after that, I don't remember exactly when, I tucked away the Zen book.

Who can blame me for my affairs with Buddhism? Aren't Buddhists beautiful? They're natural, like sand or soil, and move like the wind. Buddhists are beyond reproach. They never argue. They don't make off-color jokes or talk about the price of cars. Their every practice— even pushing a broom—is imbued with awareness. They believe a common person can become enlightened. They say wise things, like *Know when to act and when to rest.* They ask paradoxical questions, called *koans,* like *How do you climb further when you've reached the top of the highest tree?* And then—of all things—they come up with an answer.

But Judaism? It's a strange, argumentative, incomprehensible religion. It's populated by Jews, a dark and hairy people. Jews can't agree on the interpretation of their own religious laws or even decide what, exactly, constitutes a Jew. They eat strange things like congealed chicken fat on unleavened bread but forbid themselves from eating what others crave: shrimp in lobster sauce, scallops, pork loin. Bacon cheeseburgers. They use words like *shlub* and *nebbish*. They snip the tips of penises from baby boys and then celebrate. They're different from everyone else in the United States, but not in the right way.

For better or worse, secular Jews have learned to hide these differences. Cultural historian Irving Howe, in his epic book *World of Our Fathers*, predicted that this would be the case. He said that by the mid–twentieth century, Jewish life would enter an entirely new and unpredictable phase. By then, he said, the offspring of Eastern European Jewish immigrants would have achieved what he saw as the goal of secular Jews: to seem "normal" in American culture. I think we're there.

If today we aren't going to live like our grandparents, who often had the certainty of Jewish traditions, or even like our fathers and mothers, who sometimes keep the faith—then what? Then how? "Normal" American Jews still face the fundamental questions of human existence: How should we live? How can we create a moral life? Where can we encounter our spirit? Yet we lack the security of believing that Jewish laws can give us the answers. Unsatisfied, many of us turn elsewhere.

Buddhism, for example, provides its own solutions to these questions. Not too long ago, I began to wonder about Jews who turned to Buddhism. They certainly fulfilled Howe's prophecy. They represented a new phase of Judaism. Or did they?

I first heard about Jewish Buddhists when I went to see *Twitch and Shout*, a fascinating documentary about people with Tourette's syndrome. The filmmaker was at the showing and answered questions after the movie ended. When someone asked about plans for her next film, she brightened and said, "I want to make a movie about the book *The Jew in the Lotus*. It's the story of a group of Jews who went to meet the Dalai Lama. It highlights the intersections between Buddhism and Judaism. Anyone here read it? Can I see a show of hands?"

Way before she'd finished her last sentence, a collective murmur, a sort of appreciative rumble, had risen from the crowd. Hands were raised. Someone clapped. "Yeah," a voice yelled, "JUBUs."

I went out and bought the book. It raised questions. Why are Jews attracted to Buddhism? What can Judaism learn from Buddhism? Where are the points of intersection between the two religions?

One piece of dialogue in particular stayed with me. Rabbi Zalman Schachter-Shalomi, speaking about why Jews say blessings, said, "Every instinct we have can be gratified. But it always calls for stopping and becoming mindful." This rabbi, I thought, sounded like a Buddhist. But he was talking about Judaism.

I called Rodger Kamenetz, the book's author. Nervous, I opened the conversation by making a quip about the Berkeley theater crowd and asking, tongue-in-cheek, why so many Jews turned out for a film about Touretters. "Strange," I said, smiling.

"No, not strange at all," said Kamenetz, quite seriously. "A large percentage of Touretters are Jews."

The same goes for Buddhists in America. A disproportionate number are Jews. Kamenetz told me they make up a kind of distinctly American Buddhism—a Buddhism of educated white people, mainly. "Like a white-bread Buddhism?" I said.

"You could say that, yeah," he said, laughing. "Although maybe rye-bread Buddhism would be better."

His book had struck a collective chord among Jews. As one friend told another, it gathered a dedicated underground following around the country. In this way it moved through more than twenty printings—no small feat for a story about Jews on a road trip to India.

"People would come up to me at readings," Kamenetz said, marveling still, "and I'd see the book, with little yellow stickies attached everywhere, with underlinings, bent covers, the whole bit. They really read it."

So I wasn't alone in my interest. "What, exactly, do you think your book tapped into?"

"The story of Jews looking for spiritual satisfaction is ancient," he said. "That's what it's all about. We're not just talking about a group of Jews who are Buddhists. Jews have always searched. They've been the top inventors of new religions."

I could think only of Jews for Jesus. "Like what?"

"Like Christianity, for starters." He laughed. "That's a pretty successful product, if you ask me. Then too, there's Marxism, Freudianism—the top religions of the twentieth century."

Jews were searchers, that much was for sure. I recalled what his book had said about Jewish inroads into Buddhism: Jews make up between 6 percent and 30 percent of American Buddhist groups around the country. This, he said, represents up to twelve times the Jewish proportion of the American population. American Jews have founded Buddhist meditation centers and publishing houses (Shambhala Books), and have translated the religion into English. According to Kamenetz, they make up about 30 percent of the faculty teaching Buddhist studies at American universities.

What is it that drives us to look for answers outside our own traditions? Once, while on break from doing my fieldwork in Taiwan, I stayed at the Buddhist monastery on Lion's Head Mountain. Mornings, I woke to the sound of gongs, to the scratch of the futon against my back. I'd walk down a rocky mountain path to the temple, watch as monks slipped off sandals, moved inside. It was an open-air temple, a light roof held up by thin columns of bamboo. I watched. Monks sat in full lotus, stared straight ahead. They seemed to require no interaction with each other. They seemed able to be spiritual without community.

Jews are another matter. Community is central to worship. Orthodoxy, for example, requires ten men for a *minyan*, a prayer group. The other branches are less explicit in their requirement, but it's there under the surface: you have to join the fray, be engulfed by the group. As I thought about this, I realized that groups, especially ones made up of religious Jews, made me uncomfortable.

It was Emile Durkheim who said that community was an essential part of religion. Durkheim, a French sociologist, had observed Australian aborigines. He believed they reflected religion in its most elemental form. He watched their rituals. He saw the way they worshiped, how they rose together and chanted, their bodies lifting, their voices rising. Their intensity generated a heightened emotional state, one that he called *collective effervescence*. It was this energy, he said—the energy of the communal—that pushed people toward the sacred. Together, people had the power to change an ordinary moment into a sacred one.

There seemed to be so many ways to interpret religion. Durkheim said religion was a way to lift the everyday into the realm of the sacred. To me, it sometimes seemed like a structure that blew reason to the ground. It was an infinite choir of don'ts. It was a way of seeing. A body of ritual. A choice, perhaps. I had hoped it would be something that could turn me back toward myself—and then turn me outward, elsewhere, to somewhere I'd never been.

I asked Kamenetz if it was possible to be Jewish alone.

"There *is* an emphasis on community," Kamenetz said. "But there's more. Jews aren't aware of the private, individual potential for growth in Judaism. It's there. Look at the Bible. It's story after story of people on individual spiritual quests. They're in the desert; they're meditating; they're concentrating on reaching God."

He continued. "So much of Judaism is in the storehouse, unused and untapped. The *Zohar*, for example—the mystical kabbalah text—is based on meditation experiences. The book is in the form of a commentary on the Bible, the Torah. Moses, if you recall, sees the burning bush in the Torah. If you understand that as a meditation experience, it makes a lot of sense."

This was a place in Judaism that was far from where I stood. It was Judaism's spiritual center. I recalled the years I'd studied Zen shiatsu. I'd learned to move from my center, the place the Japanese call *hara*. I came to understand that hara is more than the belly. It's a concept. It has to do with wisdom, intuition, with knowing what's right. It's the midpoint of a pinwheel: in balance when all else is spinning. It's the sweet spot of a tennis racket: you know when you're there. Kamenetz made me realize I wanted to get to the hara of Judaism.

How to get there? Reading the *Zohar* in translation was about as interesting as reading the telephone book. Reading Gershom Scholem, the famous kabbalistic scholar, took me into material that was over my head. I got lost in technical details, dense language, and charts of something called *sefirot*. It vaguely reminded me of mathematics.

Kamenetz said that the spiritual, mystical aspects of Judaism are inaccessible to most Jews. These elements were suppressed by the liberal Jewish branches as far back as the German Reform movement of the nineteenth century. We've pruned our religion time and again. Vanilla Jews, most of us. The Judaism Kamenetz grew up experiencing was polite, predictable, uncomfortable with the idea of spirituality.

I opened another avenue. "Do you think," I asked Kamenetz, "that Buddhism lets JUBUs avoid their Jewishness?" My face flushed. I thought of the time in high school when someone had asked about my nationality. "Italian," I'd said. "No," I'd added, "not Jewish."

Kamenetz paused. "I can't speak for all Jews who are Buddhists. I've met some, however, who negate Judaism. These people are headed for trouble sooner or later. You can't be a whole person unless you come to some terms with your past and where you came from."

"Right." I found I was twisting the hell out of a paper clip. "I grew up embarrassed about being Jewish," I said. "Levittown was the land of no-Jews. It was better not to be too Jewish."

Kamenetz was shocked. "Too Jewish?"

"Yeah. When I think of Jews in temple, I think *pushy*. I think *noisy*." Even I could hear a strand of anti-Semitism—my own.

Kamenetz laughed. "Thank God Jews are noisy," he said, not missing a beat. "And smart. And funny—look, we've got Seinfeld, haven't we? Do the Buddhists have a Seinfeld? No. And they won't, as far as I can tell, have one soon.

"Hey," he added, teasing. "Jews are great. We're the chosen people, remember?"

I laughed, in an uncomfortable sort of way.

He talked about the way Judaism had been part of the home he'd grown up in and was now part of the home he shared with his wife and daughters. "I've always loved being Jewish," he said. While he spoke, I watched as my fingers, forcing the paper clip into contortions, finally snapped it in half.

Afterwards, I called my cousin Dylan. "How'd it go?" he asked.

"Good, but weird," I reported. "Kamenetz is great. He's smart, generous with his thoughts. He's proud to be Jewish. Emphatic about that. Toward the end of the interview, though, I started talking about my own experience of Judaism. When I told him I wasn't comfortable being Jewish, I could tell he thought I was nuts." I stopped. Dylan would tell me the truth. "Am I the only Jew with Jew-related ambivalence? Am I totally out of it?" I thought I might need a few rounds of therapy—or maybe even rebirthing.

"Are you kidding?" Dylan said. "Do you know any Jew who's *not* ambivalent?"

"What does it feel like for you to be Jewish?" I asked.

"It's like this," he said. "I never have the feeling of being sure. Being Jewish means feeling conflicted. There's no certainty about it for me."

He'd hit home. This is the predicament of nonreligious Jews: we can neither claim nor escape our Judaism. We have a problem in self-perception. A niggling, low-grade identity crisis. Howe saw this problem too. As he ended *World of Our Fathers*, he posited only two solutions for us: either a return in full to the Jewish faith or a complete abandonment of Jewish identification. Neither of these options, as it turned out, would prove viable for me.

I knew of someone who had chosen a return in full to the faith — Rabbi Alan Lew, of the Conservative congregation Beth Shalom in San Francisco. He used to be the head of the Berkeley Zen Center. Here was a man who'd traveled through many years of Zen practice only to arrive at the realization that he was irrevocably Jewish. I wanted to know about his journey. I wanted to know why he'd traded sitting zazen for davening.

Rabbi Lew had grown up in a secular Jewish family. Judaism had seemed nice, family-oriented, something akin to a minor wing of the Democratic party even — but not anything that could provide him with spiritual sustenance. When he became an adult, he looked elsewhere. He found Zen. It was love. For a decade he practiced intensely, for hours and hours each day. Then one day something inside him made itself known.

"Zen practice brings you a heightened awareness of your unconscious," he told me. We were sitting in his office, facing each other over a coffee table covered with scattered books. He leaned back in his chair. "You just sit, for long periods of time, with your breath and your posture. Your sense of your self and your mind and your unconscious becomes pretty acute. What happened was this: I realized that my unconscious material — far more than I would have guessed — was Jewish. Like white background noise. I'd go into a room and I'd be thinking, *Is this guy Jewish? Is that guy Jewish? I'm Jewish, does this guy know I'm Jewish?*"

White noise. I realized I had it too. All the time, in fact.

He leaned forward, toward me. "I was shocked to realize that this was going on in my psyche," he said. "But there it was. And the more I got a sense of myself, in this nonverbal way that you do after you've been meditating a long time, the more I began to experience myself as Jewish. I realized that being Jewish was absolutely part of who I was."

I recognized his realization. I'd heard this inner voice before. Mine had been an inconsistent voice, intruding upon my thoughts on and off for a few years in a casual sort of *Hey, I'm Jewish* way. But when the voice interrupted my first meditation in the Zen monastery, it seemed louder. It seemed like something I could no longer ignore. So I did what anthropology had trained me to do: I began watching Jews, questioning them about how they were Jewish. Always, I seemed to remain just outside the tribe.

Rabbi Lew had chosen to embrace Judaism. With that decision, a whole new path had opened up for him. "It felt like I was sort of fleshing out this map, this spiritual map that was already there," he said. "I just kept illuminating more and more facets of it."

It struck me that we shared a religion but not a faith. Where was my own map? Truly religious Jews understood their terrain. They knew which days of the week were holy, and why. They moved, square by square, in pilgrimage across the calendar, living inside days the meanings of which were foreign to me: Shabbat, Succot, Shavuot, Purim, Shemini Atzeret.

Rabbi Lew turned his head toward his bookshelf for a moment, and I caught sight of the dark skullcap cupping the back of his head. He turned to face me again, went on to explain that at thirty-five he'd entered rabbinical school, where he'd immersed himself. "That's when all that background noise, that unconscious paranoia about being Jewish, stopped. Why? Because I was directly involved."

Now he davened for hours and hours each day. He studied Torah, wrote sermons, and wrestled continuously with the rules of the faith.

I wondered about faith. Was it a small seed that grew incrementally? Or was it a decision? Did people simply get up one morning and decide to believe? Did that faith then direct the way they lived? I pictured my grandmother, leaning over the stove in the tiny kitchen of the Bronx apartment she shared with her sister-in-law.

These two old women used to light one burner before sundown every Friday so that they could cook during Shabbat.

My grandmother didn't have much patience for questions of faith. "You want to talk about faith? Who knows from faith? We leave the flame on because that's what we do. It's Saturday and so we don't turn on the gas. We turned it on already before Shabbat began." She threw up her hands. "You want other answers? Ask a rabbi. These are my answers."

Now a rabbi sat before me. "Most people don't get anything out of Judaism," he said. "You know why? Because they don't practice it in a disciplined way. But it's so obviously meant to be practiced that way. There's daily prayer, minute-by-minute practices about eating and how you conduct your business and how you conduct yourself sexually."

Rabbi Lew spoke evenly. "The religion seems so inadequate in its American presentation," he said. "Nobody even knows what a disciplined Jewish spirituality looks like. Nobody ever encounters it. What they encounter is a really washed-out, watered-down, once-a-week kind of religion that doesn't do anything, or doesn't do anything much."

The question was, *How had this watering-down occurred?* The books I'd been reading showed it wasn't just a recent American phenomenon. There was a historical precedent. As far back as the early 1800s, certain Jews in the more developed European countries suffered from self-consciousness about the way they practiced their religion. A movement began, one whose aim was to make Judaism less traditionally Jewish. German Jews were especially committed. Jews in the Hamburg temple were the first to toss out their old prayerbooks, drop references about returning to the Holy Land, avoid praying in what they deemed to be an unseemly way—a *Jewish* way. They wanted to appear genteel. They wanted to pray like the Protestants.

The movement became Reform Judaism. Jews who joined said they were looking for a way to participate in the modern world without losing their Judaism. Why not sanction a few breach-of-Shabbat prohibitions? Why not print English prayerbooks? What, really, would be lost? So began the washing-out of Judaism.

I doubted that my brand of Judaism classified as washed-out. Invisible might be closer to the truth.

I changed the subject. "What's left of your Zen experience?" I asked. "How is it reflected in the way you practice Judaism?"

"Zen taught me to live with a sense of the present," he said. "This awareness is an essential aspect of Judaism too. It's in the Hasidic teachings, in the Torah. It's the basis of Jewish religious experience. Everything in Judaism—the dietary laws and the blessings that you're supposed to say as the day progresses—is supposed to bring you to an awareness of the reality of your life. But I never could've appreciated that without Zen."

As he spoke, I realized that his sense of the moment imbued even our interview. His eyes rarely strayed from mine. He didn't blurt out answers without thinking. He spoke from his center. This meant he wasn't distracted during our discussion, although his phone rang several times and several people interrupted us. He always returned, fully engaged, to our conversation.

Rabbi Lew leaned forward again. "With *kashrut*—the Jewish dietary laws—every time you eat, you have to be conscious. This is like Zen. You have to be aware of what you're doing. And then eating becomes an act of worship." He spread his arms. "When I open up that refrigerator," he said, "what do I experience? God. God is in that refrigerator."

He held my gaze, and I understood that there was no judgment in it. It was a gaze of excitement, of interest. "Observing Shabbat, keeping kosher, these are the daily aspects of Judaism. This is ordinary Judaism. But it's precisely the ordinariness of Judaism that is its richest and most spiritual aspect."

It was Abraham Joshua Heschel who wrote, "Judaism is a religion of time, aiming at the sanctification of time." Heschel, one of the leading Jewish thinkers of the twentieth century, said that ritual, prayer, and Jewish festivals enabled us to create an architecture of time. They allowed us to delineate one moment from another. They raised our awareness of the present. My Zen cooking experience came to mind. I had the desire, but not the commitment, to achieve an intensity of awareness.

Rabbi Lew turned the conversation toward *The Jew in the Lotus*. "I'll tell you where Kamenetz and I disagree. Kamenetz says Jews are attracted to Buddhism because in Buddhism the esoteric is apparent, whereas in Judaism it's hidden. He says we need the kabbalah, the mystical aspects of Judaism, to recapture Jewish spirituality."

He shook his head, adamantly. "Not true. Buddhism isn't esoteric. It's totally fixated on mundane reality. It attunes you to the ordinary moment with almost compulsive insistence. And when you're awakened to that reality, then Judaism is a lot more attractive." He paused. "What's really needed is to open people to the spiritual richness of ordinary Judaism."

Perhaps Rabbi Lew was right.

An intercom buzz sounded the next visitor. We brought the conversation to an end. We rose, shook hands, said goodbye. Outside, I paused on the synagogue's stoop. I sat down for a moment, felt my shoulders drop. It was dusk. I watched the fog descend upon the eucalyptus trees in front of me. The air was wet, crisp, cold. I counted to three. That was when I told myself that a life is made up of small, rich moments. The ordinary is constantly revealing itself as extraordinary. God might be in my refrigerator.

I drove home slowly, reaching a darkened apartment. David was out. I draped myself over the chair. I looked at my arms. They were long, pale, somewhat muscular. I imagined wrapping one with a leather *tefillin* strap. I'd never seen a woman wearing *tefillin*, something traditionally worn by religious men. Still, I imagined encircling my arm again and again. I'd pass the strap under my nose, inhale its earthy scent. I'd pull it taut, feel it scratch against my skin.

At the end of the strap would be a small dark box containing words from the Torah. I'd bind the box against the middle of my forehead. The box would rest there, against the place Hindus call the third eye. It was a place of inner wisdom. A place of knowing. I touched the spot with my index finger. Then, there in the dark, I closed my eyes and waited.

KIKes anD queers

I was at the San Francisco Gay Lesbian Bisexual Transgender Pride Parade, and the Dykes on Bikes had just arrived in an explosion of noise. Motors — hundreds of them — revved to a thunderous pitch. People around me stamped their feet, hooted and hollered, whistled through their fingers. In the midst of the chaos a thought came to me: *names have power.*

The street was a sea of Harleys and Hondas. Topless women stopped their bikes, arched their backs like sails catching wind, raised nipples up to the sky. They preened like cats, these women, stroked the steel chests of their bikes with black-gloved fingers, held the motor's roar between their thighs. Almost everyone was tattooed. I saw a red heart resting below one woman's navel. I saw a dragon stretched across a scapula, roses blooming on biceps, a yin-yang symbol on someone's bare ankle.

After nearly an hour, the last woman arrived, slowed to a halt. A sash stretched across her chest, Miss America–style. Black cursive letters spelled *Dyke* against a white background.

D-Y-K-E. This name, with its hard consonants and abrupt end, had a power all its own. In less than a decade, the meaning of this syllable had transformed from pejorative to positive. As the woman sat back on her seat and scanned the faces around her, the crowd began chanting "Dyke, dyke, dyke." It became a mantra, an incantation, some sort of promise. *Dyke.* She waved, leaned forward, gripped the handlebars, and teased the engine. Then she was gone.

Suddenly the street was empty. I pressed forward with the rest of the crowd, craned my neck to see what was coming next. I saw three black bobbing specks several blocks down Market Street. I trained my eyes on them. They were bicycles, each one pedaled by a dark-haired man, and they were coming closer. The men took their time, swooped back and forth across the wide street. When they reached me, I saw the same sign hanging from each handlebar: *Kikes on Bikes*.

And they were, unmistakably, as advertised: kikes on bikes. The woman next to me pointed to one man, said his name was Ben Goldberg. At that moment, Ben Goldberg was smiling. The word *kike*, which usually hit me somewhere in the gut and then sank, stayed afloat. Suddenly it seemed funny. It seemed harmless. I smiled, then laughed.

They were Jews, reclaiming the word *kike*. Why not? They were queers who'd already reclaimed the word *queer*. Ever since the gay liberation movement had begun decades ago, gays and lesbians—queers, dykes—had been turning these words around. Queer was something you could call yourself. Dyke was a name you took; you said it first, preventing others from throwing it at you like a dagger. A name, sharp as a sliver of glass, can cut you. A name can cloak you, muffling the sound of truth. Or a name can be a flag, proudly announcing your presence to the world. I wanted flags. *Kike*, for one, and *Yid*. I wanted *Jew* as well, a word that sometimes made me wince.

The parade ended. I thought about origins. Where had the word *kike* begun? Years ago I'd learned that no one knew for sure. *The History of American Slang* said that the word was born on Ellis Island, when Jewish immigrants who couldn't write signed their entry forms with a circle instead of an X, a shape too close to that of a cross. The Yiddish word for circle is *kikel*, and—as the story goes—customs agents began calling *kikel!* and then *kike!* to these circle-signers. Is this a fiction? Could be. Most Jews coming from Europe could write their names.

Names. There were the names people called us, and the names we called ourselves. There were the names we kept and the names we didn't: Ralph Lifschitz (Ralph Lauren), Alan Konigsberg (Woody Allen), Melvin Kaminsky (Mel Brooks), Nathan Birnbaum (George Burns), Howard Cohen (Howard Cosell), Joseph Levitch (Jerry Lewis), Leonard Rosenberg (Tony Randall), Jean Molinsky (Joan Rivers), Herbert Solomon (Herbie Mann), Issur Danielovitch (Kirk Douglas). You know these people. They're our brothers, our sisters. And they've taken their names in vain.

Names. There were the ones we were forced to embrace. During the Holocaust, Jewish women had to take the middle name of Sara, and Jewish men had to take Israel. These names were Nazi markings; they were orders; they were a singular sort of poison. Names can dehumanize you. They can turn you into a number. They can kill you.

Names. Real Jews—the Orthodox—don't say the name of God. They spell God's name as a tetragrammaton, YHVH, something impossible to pronounce. A Lubavitch man once told me that in the time before the destruction of the second temple, only one rabbi knew how to speak God's name. Once a year people gathered to hear him voice this sound. It was the sound of the wind, of everything and nothing at all.

After the parade I went home. David had left a note saying he was out on a run. I was alone in our living room. I experimented. "Kike," I whispered, standing next to the rocker.

Then—loudly this time—I said it again. "Kike." Suddenly I thought of Ben Goldberg. I thought of Ralph Lauren and Joan Rivers. I thought about trainloads of dying Jews, and I knew their middle names were Sara or Israel. I thought of the names Moses and Benjamin, of Ruth and Esther, then Ariel and Avi, Yehuda and Yaakov. These—all of them—were my names. I carried them in my bones.

"Jew," I said, standing next to the couch.

"Yid," I said days later, when talking with a rabbi in her office. "We can take back the word. I can see it now, blazed across T-shirts."

Jane Litman, the rabbi who headed Sha'ar Zahav, the gay/lesbian/bisexual synagogue in San Francisco, laughed. She knew me. She leaned back in her chair. "Tell me more," she said.

I did. I told her that names held power. I said that as Jews, we needed to voice our names; we needed to sound them out as sacrament, as prayer. Rabbi Litman leaned forward. Her eyes held mine for a moment and I knew then that she understood: if names can be a blessing, then we must bless ourselves.

NOTES FROM THE FIELD

SEPTEMBER 1

I never learned the how-tos of keeping ethnographic field notes. Grad-school courses offered no rules, no instructions about the process. I understood it was a science of intuition. You were simply supposed to figure it out yourself—write down what you heard, what you saw, and what you thought, in the hope that sooner or later you'd see patterns emerge. If you were patient, these patterns, invisible in life, would rise up through the blue-lined notebook paper, dot the page like small beams of light. The knots and gaps of a changing culture would be there, in your lap, illuminated.

I've decided to give it a go. Why not? For a month, I'll keep field notes. The result will be a native's ethnography, a small personal anthropology of Jewishness, the way it is now, for me, for people like me, those at once ambivalent and attached to something we haven't quite figured out.

SEPTEMBER 2

I talk with Meryle Weinstein, a research associate at the Institute for Community and Religion. "The whole issue of what a Jew is," she says, "is tenuous."

Meryle feeds me the facts, according to the 1990 National Jewish Population Survey. I turn them into an index of sorts:

Estimated number of Jews in the United States: 8,190,000

Number of Jews that comprise the American "core Jewish population": 5,515,000

Number of core Jews categorized as "Jews by religion": 4,210,000

Number of core Jews categorized as "secular Jews": 1,120,000

Number of Jews outside the core Jewish population: 2,676,000

Number of "Jews by choice," a designation given to people born into another religion who now identify themselves as Jews—whether they've officially converted or not: 185,000

Percentage of Jews by choice who belong to a synagogue: 55.5

Percentage of Jews by religion who belong to a synagogue: 38.5

Percentage of secular Jews who belong to a synagogue: 5.6

SEPTEMBER 3

The numbers—what do they show? They show almost anything. They show that you can be a Jew if you call yourself a Jew. They show that some people are Jews because they go to synagogue, while others are Jews because they have Jewish blood. They show that lots of people of Jewish lineage don't identify themselves as Jews. And they show that the Jewish Population Survey can give you a headache if you stare at it long enough.

The numbers—what do they mean? They mean that millions of American Jews fall outside mainstream Judaism. That's the condition of my generation, the post-Holocaust generation of Jews. Millions answer the question of whether Judaism is religion, culture, or race with a shrug.

Religion. Culture. Race.

Synagogue. Museum. Body.

These are my vehicles to encounter Judaism, avenues at my disposal. Now for the test: Where will I truly make contact?

SEPTEMBER 4

I leave the Jewish Film Festival without getting crushed. Beforehand, I sit through a full-length movie about the Orthodox and a short about Jewish singles. Then two hundred Jews try to squeeze out the theater's double doors with me. I flatten and make it through.

Outside the doors, a bearded guy in a too-small polyester suit and a knit skullcap flags me down, shoves at me a flyer for something called the Jewish Food Festival. A *festival in celebration of Jewish, um, cuisine?* I raise my eyebrows. I don't even want to think of the ramifications.

"No thanks," I say.

I take a few strides and he dogs my heels, waves his hands, tries to peer into my face. "Yes?" he yells, two feet from my ear. "You'll come, yes? Latkes. Piroshki. Matzo brei. Saul's chicken soup. Mamelah's famous kishke. Next week. You take Highway 24 to the Broadway exit—"

I feel the heat of his breath. A voice rises within me. "Well," it says, "are we feeling Jewish yet?"

SEPTEMBER 6

Santa Cruz. David and I spend hours in bookstores, then ride the Giant Dipper twice (me screaming on the downslide, envisioning the next day's headlines: *Earthquake Topples Beachside Roller Coaster, Kills All*). We eat tostadas near the ocean, decide not to do anything as ambitious as swimming and instead fall asleep on the beach, legs entwined like curled limbs of driftwood.

Dinner at India Joze. We order tofu and taro root, soft things, entrées with made-up Indonesian names. Lots of peanut sauce. Then David opens his mouth, steps unknowingly into enemy territory.

"I've been thinking," he says casually. "It's actually kind of odd, the way your writing—the stuff you've shown me recently—keeps focusing on being Jewish." He spears a tofu cube with his chopstick.

"What do you mean?" The back of my neck tenses.

"Well," he continues. Munch. Spear. Munch. "You don't go to temple." Munch. Spear. "You don't observe the Sabbath. You don't even celebrate the major holidays. Remember—I was the one who wanted to go to the Passover seder last year. You bagged out at the last minute, so we didn't go."

The broccoli head. Fake to the left. Spear. "But your writing makes it sound as though Judaism is important, as though it's a focus of yours in everyday life."

"It is." My hand closes in on my napkin, clenches the fabric.

"Really?" He looks at me.

"Yeah."

He shrugs. "Whatever you say. I just don't see it. I don't see any evidence."

"Evidence?"

"Right. You're not religious. You don't even belong to a Jewish cultural organization. You're not a member anywhere. It's like your Judaism is invisible."

I lean forward over the table. I raise my voice. "The way I spend my days doesn't express my thoughts. Going to temple wouldn't make me more of a Jew. And the last time I checked, I didn't need a membership card for this tribe. I was born into it."

I'm pissed off. David looks baffled. "Wait. Look. I'm not trying to start a fight. I just want to understand your relationship to Judaism."

I know he's first rewinding and then fast-forwarding the conversation in his head, searching for clues, wondering, *Where was the landmine? What did I say wrong?*

But it wasn't what he said. It's what I thought I heard; it's the thought behind his words; it's what I projected—*You aren't a convincing Jew.*

He'd hit a sore spot. I stab at my bits of Bo Lop beef. I wonder if he's right.

Would going to temple be proof of a commitment to Judaism? I'd guess that many people in any given religious service spend time daydreaming. Some think about what they're going to make for dinner or worry about their next paycheck. Some probably can't explain why they go to services at all. Perhaps it's a habit, like doing sit-ups in the morning. Perhaps it's a form of solace, like sitting with old friends. But is it always evidence of religious commitment? Of a struggle for religious meaning? Of being a True Jew? No.

I say none of this. Dinner comes and goes. Half-eaten plates of noodles are exchanged for a check. I'm in a funk. In the silence of our drive back home, it occurs to me that my thoughts are rarely visible. Mostly they grow and change and shed as invisibly as layers of skin.

SEPTEMBER 8

I find this quote in *The Book of Questions*, by Edmond Jabès.

My brothers turned to me and said: "You are not Jewish. You do not go to the synagogue."

I turned to my brothers and answered: "I carry the synagogue within me."

SEPTEMBER 10

My parents will be in town for Rosh Hashanah. I decide to take them to a service. This could be a problem:

1. I don't belong to a temple.

2. My mother has never been to a high holy day service.

3. My father hasn't gone since he was forced as a boy.

When my mother calls, I ask her if she'll go.

"A service?" she says. "All of a sudden you want to observe Rosh Hashanah? Why?"

She pauses, asks suspiciously, "Are you going through some kind of religious Jewish phase?"

I get the phone number of Aquarian Minyan, the Jewish Renewal congregation in Berkeley. Jewish Renewal is a relatively new branch of Judaism. They claim a spiritual, politically aware, nonsexist, creative interpretation of Judaism.

The woman at the other end of the line tells me there are still spaces left for Rosh Hashanah services. She mentions that I should bring a drum if I have one. I reserve four seats even though I can already picture my mother's raised eyebrows.

SEPTEMBER 13

The Claremont Hotel, room 202. My mother is wearing perfume. When I tell her that Aquarian Minyan's flyer discourages wearing perfume at the service to protect the health of people with chemical sensitivities, she rolls her eyes.

"I can tell already what this night will be like," she says. "Can't we just go to a movie and forget about Rosh Hashanah?"

She grabs the flyer from me and reads aloud: "'Pillows will be provided for those who want to sit on the floor.' Pillows? For the floor?"

She looks down at the tailored skirt and elegant jacket she's wearing. Then she laughs. "Murray," she yells to my father in the other room, "I think we're going to be a bit overdressed for this one."

David arrives at the hotel a half-hour late, gripping a cup of coffee. I see the coffee as a mild insult. Does he expect to fall asleep? We pile into the car. Everyone is too conscious that we're going to a religious service. My father says something about the oppressive nature of organized religion. The car should have a placard attached — *Warning: Three Uncomfortable Jews and a Lapsed Unitarian. Contents Under Pressure.* My mother asks why Jewish services are going to be held at a Unitarian Church.

"Because the Jews own everything," David says, "even the Unitarians."

They banter until we stop at a light near the UC Berkeley campus. From a herd of students crossing the street emerge two Orthodox Jewish men. The men walk in front of us, a slow-motion detail of Jewish life. I see everything: their overgrown beards and black curls, their prayer-shawl fringes hanging beneath jackets, their dark-skinned hands grasping prayerbooks, their unabashed Jewishness. The juxtaposition is jarring. My family lacks a sense of necessity about the evening's activity. It's an elective, a novelty. Our voices cease as we stare. These men are a sign of some sort. They're my conscience.

David breaks open the moment. "Ixnay on the ew-jay jokes," he says, gangster-like, out of the side of his mouth. Who knows why, but I laugh. Then the light changes and we're off.

The church is jammed. Most people are in loosely flowing cotton clothes. Luckily, no one is wearing beads. One guy, inevitably, is in tie-dye. I see a sign for a scent-free zone and steer my mother past it quickly. We find seats in front of a nice man resting his arm on a congo drum. He invites us to use it whenever we want. My parents are charmed.

Because this congregation has no rabbi, practiced laypeople lead the service. It begins with a request for all congregants to introduce themselves to those around them. David and I say hello to a few people and smile politely. Then I stare straight ahead until David nudges me.

"Look at your folks," he says. "It's like they've been coming here for years."

I turn. They're leaning forward, then backward, then to either side, talking at great length to everyone around them. Now they're laughing, clasping the hands of the couple next to them. I have to shush them when the service begins. My parents are having a Jewish renaissance.

"Go light a candle for your sister," my mother says.

She points toward the front, where people are lined up, waiting their turn. She doesn't finish the rest of her sentence, which I know includes the words, *Pray that she meets a guy*.

"Aren't those candles for the dead?" I ask. I haven't a clue.

"How should I know?" she snaps in a whisper.

Bewildered, we look at each other. Neither of us makes a move toward the line. We don't want to screw up my sister's chance at a relationship by lighting a candle meant for the dead. In silent defeat, my mother waits for the next part of the service to begin.

One of the lay leaders begins to speak about the coincidence of Rosh Hashanah falling on Shabbat this year. She tells us to close our eyes, to breathe deeply. Then she says that Shabbat is a time of perfection.

"It's a time to suspend judgments of yourself," she says. "Know that you are perfect. That each of you, during Shabbat, is utterly perfect. From now until the sun sets tomorrow." I close my eyes and in a few minutes am surprised by a sense of peace.

"I encourage you all to get up during this next prayer," she says. "Dance, if you're moved to."

She picks up her guitar to sing, and people begin to sing with her. Lines of people rise without hesitation, join hands, move to the front and sides of the church and sway in an impromptu dance. I look at David, who shakes his head vigorously no and is about to tell me why when my parents rise.

"Up, up, up—David, get up," my mother says, and he's too surprised to say no, too surprised to do anything but be swept along into the hands of the people waiting.

Later, when we're seated, we read aloud from the prayerbook. Most of the prayers are in Hebrew with a transliteration, which means I can pronounce words but have no idea of their meaning. During the English prayers I'm confronted with the word *God* again and again. I can't pray to God—I'm not sure I believe in God—so I substitute the words *our highest selves*. That'll work for now.

The service goes on and on. We shift back and forth on our butts. We look around for a sign, any sign, that the end might be near. No such luck. David points to his watch. It's nine o'clock, and none of us has eaten dinner. We nod to each other. We know our limit. We get up. We file out of the pew, down the aisle, and out the door.

At home later, David and I are in bed. He runs his fingers lightly over my forehead. "Remember what the woman said about the Sabbath?" he says. "I loved that. Maybe we can try not to judge each other for one day every week. For the Sabbath. We won't judge each other and we won't judge ourselves."

I hug him tightly. I don't say, of course, what the truth is: we'll remember this pact for a few days, then slip back into imperfection, into being flawed humans. That's life. That's how it is.

SEPTEMBER 14

Breakfast at the Claremont Hotel. My parents and I are rating yesterday evening's synagogue service.

"Um, I'd say a five," I ventured.

"Maybe a six," says my father.

"Did you see some of those outfits? Vay. From the last century," my mother says.

"It was more interesting than I expected," says my father.

"Mom? Final verdict?"

She's buttering her toast. "It was quaint."

"Quaint? You're calling a holy religious service *quaint?*"

"Mmm."

I look at my father. "Dad? Did you like it?"

He smiles but it's a halfway job, strained, closer to a grimace. "There were a few nice parts. I liked the music, the singing. And I liked the people. To me, Judaism is about people. I like Jewish people. I liked that we were all together. But the service itself?" He shrugs. "What can I say? It seems foolish. The whole thing. The rituals, the prayers, the believing in God."

My mother clears her throat. She ends the conversation with the crucial question: "How much," she says, "did you have to pay for those tickets?"

September 16

My parents and I are driving to the Jewish Museum to see *Too Jewish: Challenging Traditional Identities,* a museum installation curated by Norman Kleeblatt. The exhibit probes the question of what it means to be Jewish—or *too* Jewish—in America. Kleeblatt had traveled around, observing the margins of the Jewish art scene, and began to notice themes emerging from the work: a preoccupation with the Holocaust, a self-consciousness about the ethnic body, a desire to reinvent ritual, an alienation from popular mainstream culture. Picking and choosing, he ended up with a brash, in-your-face collection of work that commented on the complicated, fractured state of Jewish identity today. The artists were mostly third- or fourth-generation American Jews.

In preparation for our museum visit, my parents and I read the

San Francisco Chronicle's article about the exhibit and take note: there's an entire wall devoted to noses. Jewish noses.

In the car, I bring up something that's been nagging me. "I noticed," I say to my mother, "that your nose used to be smaller. In all the old photos."

"Thanks, sweetheart," she says, patting my knee. "Now I feel really terrific." She doesn't miss a beat, though. She tells me I'm right. Then she gives me a rundown of every nose, Jewish and non-Jewish, in the family. She also tells me about a friend of hers who had two nose jobs. "She had the first one, and I didn't notice the difference. For a year, every time she asked, I said it looked great. Then one day she sat me down and said, 'Tell me the truth, can you see the difference between this nose and the last one?' What could I say? I said no. She thanked me and said she was going to get another one." My mother pauses. "So what happens? Second time: same doctor, same nose. Same exact nose. Can you believe this?

"And have I told you about the girl Dad and I met at the hospital?" she asks. I shake my head no. "The girl was in bed alone so we began to talk with her. She was waiting to get her second nose job. Her parents wouldn't come to the hospital because they disapproved of the operation. They told her there was nothing wrong with her nose. You know why they said this? *Because there was nothing wrong with her nose.*" She stops, turns to my father in the back seat. "You remember, hon? Am I exaggerating?" My father corroborates the story. "This girl was stunning. Perfect. When we told her she was beautiful, she became very upset with us. She said she hated her nose. She had to change it."

My mother pauses, stares straight ahead. "Crazy. This world is crazy," she says. Then she turns to me. "And you? You have a nice nose. A lovely nose, compared to Dad and me. But honey, it'll grow. So what? That's what happens eventually. What can you do? Nothing. Your nose grows and your lips thin." She laughs. "So that's what you have to look forward to."

I can't look at my mother just then, because for some reason I'm overcome by a surprising swell of love.

At the museum, we see Seth Kramer's video. He's a guy who visits one of the Polish camps with several Holocaust survivors. Then he talks about the experience. He says he's read about the Holocaust for many years and thought he understood something about it. But when he steps into the camps he realizes he's been wrong. Reading about the Holocaust doesn't equal understanding it. His face in the video registers an awesome mix of sadness, disgust, fear, anxiety, incomprehension, and pensiveness.

After he returns to the States he becomes obsessed with the number 6,000,000. How can someone fathom what that number really means? First he figures out how old he'd be if he lived to be 6,000,000 hours old. His friends and relatives guess: "One hundred years old?" they ask. Wrong. The answer, which surprises even him, is six hundred years.

He wants to get still closer to the number 6,000,000. He doesn't want this figure to continue to be an abstraction. He decides to count, one by one, 6,000,000 grains of rice. Counting rice grains will take a month or two of his free time, he figures. The video juxtaposes clips of him counting tiny grains of rice at his kitchen table against torn-off calendar pages and handwritten tabulations of his progress. January goes by. Then February and March. After nine months his table is covered with more than fifteen jars of every possible size filled with rice. "This," he says, his hand extending across the table, "represents only one million grains. It took me nine months to count this far." He shakes his head in amazement. "I guess I'll be starting with the children. The Nazis killed one and a half million children. After I'm finished counting the rice that represents those kids, I'll move to the adults. It may take me years."

The video cuts to an interview with an SS officer. The Nazi tells the camera that he was in charge of a special gas chamber. "What was so unusual about it?" the interviewer asks.

"It was the best one ever built," he says. "It could exterminate up to three thousand Jews in three hours."

For the rest of the day I wonder how I can live in a world where killing people sounds so much easier than counting rice.

SEPTEMBER 20

I arrive at the hotel a half-hour later than my parents had requested. This means that we get to the airport two and a half hours instead of three before their flight departs.

We stand curbside at the American Airlines terminal while a baggage guy darts around us, tagging bags. My parents suddenly look very small. Vulnerable, like they could be knocked over accidentally at any minute by this baggage guy. I stop myself from telling them to be careful.

My mother usually cries when we part. Now she's fluttering around me, worrying about my drive home, reminding me not to daydream at the wheel, brushing invisible hairs from my shoulder. She hugs me hard, her hug not at all like that of a small woman. This time, when she steps back, I'm the one who's crying.

My father hugs me next, whispers in my ear two of his truths. "Just be happy," he says, "because it all goes so quickly. Worry less about tomorrow."

I get in the car and roll down the window. My mother cups a hand around her mouth. She yells her last bit of wisdom. "And get pregnant already," she says. "We can't wait around forever."

SEPTEMBER 22

It's Yom Kippur, a day of fasting. The real Jews will be in synagogue today, hungry and devout. David begs off when I ask him if he wants to go to services, ends up shooting pool. I'm on my own.

I head for a particular Reform service in San Francisco. Why there? Economics. Simple mathematics. I can afford the entry fee of that congregation. Forget about going to most services in this city. It's a major investment. You need to save up for it or you need to use Visa, so you can at least get the airline mileage.

These Jews are meeting at a Unitarian Church too. We start the service by standing, introducing ourselves to the people on either side of us, and singing the words of a Hebrew prayer. I try to stay in the moment but I can't follow the tune, don't feel connected to the meaning of the prayer. An emotional swell of voices surrounds me.

The pew feels particularly hard. The prayers seem particularly long. The rabbi finally stands up at the platform and begins his speech. I bristle. He's moralizing. He's sermonizing. The people around me are rapt.

Hours pass. Each one is interminable; it's a kind of spiritual torture, a holy rack. Voices begin inside my head:

"You can leave if you want."

"No, you can't."

"Leave. You showed up. You tried. It ain't working."

"Don't leave. It's rude. It's wrong. It's incomplete."

"I'm leaving."

"Go ahead then. You've failed. I can't say exactly how, but you've failed."

I get up. I make my way out of my row. I leave. Two and a half hours is more than enough. My lower spine feels crushed and sore, as if I've just hauled a boulder. I'm hungry. I'm suddenly irritated. Why should I fast? Who am I kidding? Screw it. I head for the car.

I floor it to Paco's Taqueria. In my long black skirt and cream silk blouse I stand at the counter. I'm ridiculous here but don't have time to dwell on that fact. I have five seconds to shout my order.

"A black-bean burrito with extra guacamole and hot sauce."

"What?" Paco cups his hand over an ear. He can't hear me. Pots and pans, or maybe giant spatulas, are crashing to the floor somewhere nearby.

"A Super Bean, extra guac, extra hot," I yell.

Crash. Silence.

"Gracias."

In seconds, the two-pound aluminum-wrapped Super appears on my tray. I carry it to the nearest booth, where I sit, my elbow suddenly wet in someone else's bean juice, and eat my burrito, bite by bite, very much alone.

SEPTEMBER 24

I go back to the Jewish Museum. I want to see the exhibit again. It has something to do with the tension there. The raw energy in each piece of art, the edge, the tongue-in-cheekness of it all wakes up something inside me. The stereotypes—the LOUDNESS of the Jewishness there—fascinate me, make me confront my own discomfort, my own internal tensions.

I'm dwarfed by Barbra Streisand's nose, in profile, which is larger than life. Four silk-screened head-shots of Streisand are repeated, Warhol-style, on an enormous canvas entitled *Four Barbras*. I take it all in and then move on to *Chanel Hanukkah*, a quilted gold Chanel handbag that Cary Leibowitz and Rhonda Lieberman turned into a menorah. It'd make any Jewish American princess preen. The artists attached nine Chanel lipstick holders to the top of the bag. I move on again, then stop dead in my tracks in front of Cary Leibowitz's six-foot-high billboard. Blue and red letters on a white background seem to yell, like some big fat shmegegge in the Catskills you want to turn from:

I'M
A
JEW
HOW
'BOUT
U?!!

Then I find Beverly Naidus's photocopies. She culls all-American magazine ads from the 1950s and 60s, photocopies them, and overlays her own text. In *What Kinda Name Is That?* I see an ad with four pajamaed teenage girls at a slumber party. I know immediately that none of the girls is in the least Jewish. All of them, I can tell, go to school at Saint Mary's Junior High or perhaps at The Virgin Mother. They're debs, spoiled and pert. Here's the text that Naidus lays like an indictment over the ad:

> She comes home from summer camp ashamed of
> her curly hair.
>
> All the hip campers had long, straight hair à la Joan Baez.
> She buys a hair straightening product
> and suffers through the stench and sting of it.
> It only works for a while.
>
> Her next effort is wrapping her hair in curlers the size of
> orange juice cans.
> Bobbie pins become embedded in her scalp as she struggles
> to sleep.
>
> Finally her cousin teaches her how to iron her hair.
> The smell of it burning reminds her of something so
> horrible,
> it is unspeakable.

I take it all in and then move on, ending up once again in front of Dennis Kardon's wall of noses. Because the noses aren't attached to faces—they're stuck up against the white wall like a collection of scientific specimens—they look strange, abstract. When no one is looking, I feel my own nose. I imagine sculpting it and try to understand its shape. I tug on the sides gently, trace the outline of its ridges and peaks. My nose is a mountain.

The Jewish look. The body—our noses, our hair, our shape, our coloring, everything—has always haunted us. Why? Are we people of the book or people of the body? Again and again, what are we? Religion? Race? Culture? Again and again, we are all three. This and more.

SEPTEMBER 26

The rain is merciless. It pelts me, lays my hair flat as a wet bed of grass, runs mascara down the sides of my face. So much for appearances. I have to meet a client soon, someone who wants me to write copy for a Website. I'm supposed to look clean, neat, together. I'm worried. I need a hot chocolate with whipped cream.

The guy working the Pasqua cart is tall and black and irrepressible. He hums as he squirts the syrup into my cup, shouts to the regulars. "Hey, Joe," he yells to someone over my shoulder, "how's that beautiful baby boy of yours?"

Back to humming. He tops my chocolate with a peak of white cream and hands me the cup. I notice a flash of gold on his wedding finger.

"Your ring," I say, "it's beautiful." And it is.

He beams, thrusts out his hand for my inspection. "So's my marriage. Twenty-one years." He holds his hand up as though reading from it and recites something that sounds almost—but not exactly—like Hebrew.

"It's Hebrew," he says. "You see these letters etched into the ring? *I am my beloved's and my beloved is mine.* Married a nice Jewish girl from Brooklyn. Hey—" he looks into my face. "You're Jewish, aren't you? Shalom, sister." He gives me a half-bow. "Shabbat shalom, baby. My name's Tasad. I'm a Muslim. Who says Jews and Muslims can't get along? Wrong! I know the truth. You're Jewish, right? Right?"

It takes me a minute. "Uh. Yeah." I smile, nod my head vigorously to make up for the lapse. "How'd you know?"

"Sister, you know how it is." He shrugs. "You've got that look, baby." I pull out two bills and try to hand them over. He waves them away. "Nope. Can't hear of it. Not today—today it's on me. It's Friday. It's Shabbat, ain't it? Shabbat shalom, sister." He winks. "Peace, from Tasad."

He looks over my shoulder at the man behind me. "Now, Joe, your turn. You tell me again, my man: How's that beautiful baby boy of yours? I hope you brought me pictures."

SEPTEMBER 27

The reference librarian hands the book to me gingerly. It's a relic of the thirties held together by tape gone brittle. The book, a scholarly work written by Harvard anthropologist Carleton Stevens, is called *The Races of Europe*. I look up Jews in the index and find this:

> The feature which confirms the tentative identification of a person as a Jew, aside from clothing, speech, and other external cultural phenomena, is a characteristic facial expression centered about the eyes, nose, and mouth. Not all Jews, by any means, have it; those who lack it may be just as "Jewish" in the racial sense as those that possess it. . . .

When I'm finished reading, I hand the book back to the librarian just as gingerly as I received it. The paragraph follows me home. I stand in the bathroom, in front of the mirror, where the light is best. Then I lean into my reflection and stare at my face for a long, long time.

SEPTEMBER 28

Mark McCormick, a Web client, confides that for a long time he's been thinking seriously of converting to Judaism. Ever since he was thirteen, a boy in Pocatello, Idaho, reading Chaim Potok, he's felt the pull. I meet his boyfriend—a man who isn't Jewish, yet seems to know more about Jewish history than I ever could. He and Mark take me to Saul's, the Jewish deli in Berkeley. We eat hot pastrami together. They take turns telling me about a particularly beautiful bar mitzvah they'd attended. Mark says he believes Jews are special. When that remark stops my fork in midair, he laughs. Then he looks at me for a long moment, as one might look at a painting, and I understand that we'll be friends.

The next day Mark emails me a Yehuda Amichai poem. The poem speaks to me. It says, *Where do I contact myself as a Jew?*

Poem Without an End

> Inside the brand-new museum
> there's an old synagogue.
> Inside the synagogue
> is me.
> Inside me
> my heart.
> Inside my heart
> a museum.
> Inside the museum
> a synagogue,
> inside it
> me,
> inside me
> my heart,
> inside my heart
> a museum.

SEPTEMBER 30

Historically, anthropologists have been loath to publish their field notes. They're often too personal, too honest, a tad too unscientific. They show a hodgepodge—stories and scenes, conversations, facts and figures, questions, confusion—a collection of stuff, evidence of what it means to be a cultural observer. They show stray thoughts, character flaws like impatience and self-righteousness. I love the story of the esteemed English anthropologist Evans-Pritchard, who, upon arrival in the southern Sudan for fieldwork among the Nuer, became furious that none of these natives, who had most likely never seen a thing like luggage before, would carry his bags.

Field notes. They're supposed to show patterns. They're supposed to reveal the societal underpinnings, magnify our smallest actions into larger meanings. How? When I look back over my own notes of the past month and try to pick out patterns, I find none. It's too soon, perhaps. I must look at my notes as beginnings, gossamer strands to weave together slowly as time goes on.

I close my eyes, run my fingers over my notes. I touch the words, touch myself. Skin touches skin—the skin of the page, the skin of my body. Page. Body. Word. Body. Judaism.

Me and you: the observer and the observed. Who is enlightening whom? I want to say this, right now, right here: we can help each other.

There will be no secrets. There will be no rules. Take these notes in your hands. Touch my letters; run your hands across my black marks. Tell me what you find. I'm sure I've missed something important. Whatever you see, tell me. And I'll tell you. I'll keep telling you. We'll tell each other. And through each other, we'll find ourselves. That's how it works.

jUDaism: THE BranD

1 landed another Web project. This one was a good gig with a big firm—three months of brainstorming and a twenty-page deliverable. My client, which designed men's sportswear, wanted to know how to migrate their brand, their public image, to the Web. They hired me as their Internet brand strategist.

It was time to produce. Before the site was sketched out—architected, in Web lingo—I was supposed to analyze their audience, their brand, their needs, their competition, and their marketing goals. Then I was to create a strategy, write a plan for moving forward.

I tried. I sat in front of the computer. I typed *The Audience* near the top of the screen. I told myself to write about smooth-skinned men who drove SUVs, traveled abroad once a year, and shaved with a Braun. I told myself to write about the ways in which men as consumers were traditionally brand-loyal. Then I placed my fingers on the keyboard. Nothing. Judaism kept getting in the way, dominating my thoughts. Brand loyalty. Judaism. Brand loyalty. Judaism. Jews. Jews. Jews.

My father's mantra ran through my head. *Religion is a business.* I'd heard the line so often in the past that it had lost power. Now it struck me anew. I toyed with it, turned it over. If Judaism was a business, then it had an image, it had a market, it had competition, a tagline even. If Nike's tagline was *Just Do It,* then what was Judaism's? *The Chosen Ones?* I cringed. We could do better.

I gave up on men's sportswear. I cleared the screen. I hit the keys. I typed the following.

Jew Inc. USA: The Brand Identity

The Problem

American Judaism is losing market share, especially among third-generation Jews, the post-assimilation generation. Ironically, these Jews represent the very market segment that can bring new life to this ancient business, now suffering from an outdated brand.

The Solution

The brand needs updating. It needs an influx of creative energy. For starters, the tagline, an essential component of any brand, needs to be reenvisioned.

The Tagline

Informal polling of the target audience reveals negative responses to *The Chosen Ones*. A sampling of results:

"Embarrassing."

"Arrogant."

"Doesn't reflect how I feel."

"Chosen? For what—the Holocaust? Get real."

Judaism needed a new tagline. Clearly, *The Chosen Ones* wasn't working. It was too biblical. Too ambiguous. Definitely not something to splash across a billboard. I needed expert advice. I called another brand strategist, my friend Ruby Lowenstein, for starters.

"Think in taglines," I said, "for Judaism. Let's get rid of *The Chosen Ones*. Start with Microsoft's ad campaign. Can you do a knockoff? Can you work from their slogan, *Where do you want to go today?*"

"Hmmm." Then silence. I heard her fingers hit the keys. "Got it. Picture this. An enormous billboard. A gigantic piece of gefilte fish. And then the question, *What do you want to eat today?*"

"Perfect," I said. "We could do a whole series. First it'll be gefilte fish. Then—three matzo balls in a bowl of broth. *What do you want to eat today?*"

"Sounds great." Ruby cupped her hand over the phone for a moment and then returned. "I have to cut this short, sweetheart. My ten o'clock is on his way."

I phoned David at work. "Babe," I said, "think tagline. Think Judaism. Steal from the best. Work from your favorite slogans and revise."

He sighed. "I suppose it doesn't matter that I have a design due today? That I have a client waiting?"

"Judaism calls. Please."

He put me on hold.

"All right," he said when he picked back up. "How about Apple's *Think Different* campaign? We change it to *Pray Different*. We splash the tagline over an image of—not Gandhi, like Apple did, but Freud. Not Lucille Ball but Gilda Radner. We use Einstein's image. We enlarge the faces of dozens of different Jewish luminaries on billboards across the city. *Pray Different* runs across the top of each."

These were great. Still, I wanted more.

"More?" He hit the hold button again. I tapped my feet.

"I'm ready," he said, picking back up. "Think of Altoids. Their tagline: *Curiously Strong Mints*. Now picture their ad. I know you've seen it. This guy, all muscles, is leaning over, his biceps flexed, palming an Altoid tin. Got it? Okay. Here's the Jewish twist. Envision the ad, maybe a billboard. Instead of the muscle guy, we feature Sandy Koufax. Or—hey, we could show Alan Greenspan, Golda Meir. They're flexing their biceps. And the tagline?"

He paused for dramatic effect. "*Jews. A Curiously Strong People.*"

"Love it." I said. "Now do one more. Please? Think of the Nike campaign. *Just Do It*."

He didn't even pause. "*Just Jew It*."

Event promotions. Co-branding. These were the next steps, the best ways to create awareness for a brand. Kodak sponsors 10k runs. Budweiser sponsors triathlons. And Judaism? What would we sponsor—therapy sessions?

I imagined Judaism sponsoring the New York City Marathon. I saw the Orthodox Crown Heights Lubavitchers in full garb, handing out free samples of matzo brei at the finish line. Television cameras captured them there, embracing Joan Benoit Samuelson, giving her a paper plate weighted down at the center by oily bricks of brei.

Judaism needed, at the very least, an ad campaign. What did we have now? Full-page ads in the *New York Times* against interfaith marriage. They showed a doomsday scenario, the estimated rate of decline in Jews worldwide if intermarriage continued at its present rate. The whole ad campaign depressed me. It pointed fingers.

I reached down, pulled a magazine from beneath my desk. I paged through, stopped at a Marlboro ad. Over decades, Marlboro had carefully crafted a brand identity. On the page in front of me, two Marlboro Men, blue-jeaned and comfortably weathered, traded smokes on the plains. Words like *manly, strong, enduring* came to mind. The ad made smoking cigarettes look like a wilderness activity, something akin to horseback riding. If Marlboro could work this magic with a nightmare like cigarettes, then why couldn't Jews do the same with the image of Judaism in pop culture?

Jews are funny. This much is true. So why shouldn't we use humor? On my windowsill was an empty bottle of He' Brew beer, a microbrew produced in the Bay Area. Their label is awesome. A green-faced Hasid in an orange hat ecstatically holds high his hands, a beer bottle in each one. The copy: *After 3000 years of civilization, finally a microbrew with the chutzpah to call itself The Chosen Beer.*

My eyes fell back to the magazine in front of me. I flipped through the pages, saw an ad for the newest *Die Hard* movie. There was Bruce Willis, driving off a cliff. Didn't he drive off an edge in his last movie as well? No—maybe that was *Thelma and Louise*. It didn't matter. None of them was Jewish.

When was the last time I'd seen a Jew lead an action movie? (When was the first time?) Who were our powerful leading men, our studs? We didn't have Harrison Ford, Tom Cruise, John Travolta, or Mel Gibson. We didn't have James Bond. We had—Woody Allen. He was our star, our brand identity in Hollywood.

I saw Woody going up against Arnold Schwarzenegger in *The Terminator*. Arnold, caught in a corner, twists, turns, finds himself looking down at our hero. Woody glares, makes his hands into fists, stands on tiptoe. No go. He grimaces. Something's wrong.

He can't even reach Arnold's chin.

"Hold on a minute," he says, pulling over a chair on which to stand.

In *Building Strong Brands*, David Aaker said that updating a brand is difficult, especially for heritage brands such as Hallmark or Quaker Oats. The challenge for these brands, he said, is *to gradually evolve, to become more contemporary while still being familiar*. In other words, you couldn't give Aunt Jemima a full makeover overnight. Consumers would revolt. They could handle only incremental changes—a hair trim, a hint of fresh color on her cheeks. Over time, Auntie could gradually change. She could, as Aaker phrased it, *evolve an identity*.

Judaism was a kind of heritage brand. And I was trying to evolve my own identity—cultural, religious, and spiritual. Today, though, I was looking for affirmation outside, in magazines, on the big screen. I shifted in my seat. Why was I trying to brand something that was beyond branding? Even the word *branding* had complex connotations when attached to Judaism, to Jews—a people who had been, in the past, physically and socially branded as undesirable, a people who'd once had six-pointed stars sewn on their clothes and numbers tattooed on their forearms.

This was the world. It was a place where little white mints came in strong tins and Aunt Jemima had to move slowly. This was evolution, I supposed. I leaned forward, closed the magazine.

STRAY HAIRS AND PAINTED NAILS

I wanted immersion. It was a water thing. A ritual dating back three thousand years. It was something that reached the upper limits of that state of being I'd call *very Jewish*.

The *mikvah*: a ritual bath. I knew it was out there, this core Jewish experience, waiting for me. I thought of it as a womb, as the Jewish version of rebirthing. It was a container of liquid holiness, a path to instant transformation, a wash of God. It was a sure thing, a straight shot to another realm. I wanted in. I was searching for the sacred, and I was attracted—although I wouldn't admit it—to things exotic. Wasn't the exotic a sure path to transformation?

My short-term therapist bristled. "Mikvah? Why go there? Isn't it a ritual based on the premise that women are unclean? Polluted even? I've got a problem with that perspective." She peered at me over her glasses.

My cousin Dylan was equally adamant. He raised his voice, startling the people next to us in the hot tub at Orr Hot Springs, a retreat way up in the small-town hills of northern California. Orr is all about water. You move from tub to tub, warm pool to warm pool, until your body finally goes limp.

Dylan lifted his head from the side of the tub, slapped his hand against the water for emphasis. "Jews are freaks. This proves it. We hold onto these weird, ancient, convoluted practices, like mikvah.

Holy dunking? In a blessed tub? With every specification—the dimensions of the tub, the number of stairs, the water temperature, the way you dunk—every detail measured out to God's orders? And hello, like it really went from God's mouth to someone's ear? I've heard that you can't touch the walls of the tub when you immerse or the whole moment's moot. It's nuts. Admit it."

"No comment," I said. I leaned back, let a warm rush of water close over my face. Immersion. I would renew myself. The mikvah ritual would be exotic, a sort of baptism, a dip in the Ganges.

Everywhere, water was understood as a necessity for life. It *was* life. It flowed; it froze; it sprang from the sky, seeped into the earth, and rose up again. Water—to Christians, Jews, Yorubas, and Hindus, to religious people around the world—had the power to transform. How could it transform me?

The mikvah. I'd learned of it only recently, from a frayed paperback, *The Ritual Bath*, by Faye Kellerman. In a used bookstore near my house, I'd plucked it from a pile, turned to the back cover:

Someone has declared unholy war on the holiest of places. ... The quiet ordered world of a yeshiva in the California hills is shattered by an unspeakable crime: a woman is brutally raped as she returns from the mikvah, the bathhouse where women perform their cleansing ritual.

Call me lame. Call me a victim of schlock back-jacket copy, but I was hooked. I bought it, went home. I threw myself on the couch with the book and a bag of chocolate almonds, devouring both in the course of an afternoon. Surprise: I quickly found that it wasn't the crime that compelled me through the narrative. It was the notion of mikvah. I read hurriedly through the plot, searching for passages about the practice, the pleasure, the prohibitions, the religious reasoning behind it all.

How could she begin to explain the importance of the ritual bath—how integral it was to all of Judaism? The rainwater pool was the symbolic essence of Taharat Hamishpacha—family purity. Its waters were used to cleanse the dead spiritually, and immersion in it was essential before a non-Jew could be converted. Even the cooking and eating utensils made of metal were dunked to render them clean. Mikvah was a mainstay of Jewish life—as much a part of Orthodoxy as dietary laws, circumcision, or the Sabbath.

It was in this way, through Kellerman, that I learned the basics. Apparently, the most important and consistent use of mikvah has been to purify a menstruating married woman. Jewish law says that from the time her cycle begins and for seven days after it ends—at which time she enters the mikvah waters—a woman can't have a roll in the hay, make the willow weep with her husband. No petting, necking, caressing. No licking. No touching. Why? Because a woman who's bleeding is called *niddah*, which means separated. She's unholy, impure, able to pass contamination. She's a threat to the spiritual balance of her domestic heterosexual world.

I learned that men, too, go to the mikvah. The men in Kellerman's book, bearded Orthodox figures scurrying from home to shul and back again, sometimes immersed before Shabbat and holidays, before morning prayers, and on their wedding day.

The mikvah is a sacred place, a sunken Roman bath exactly four feet deep and seven feet square. According to Jewish law, at least two hundred gallons of the water in the bath must have emanated from a natural, divine source like a river, ocean, or lake. Rain, snow, ice— Rina, the mystery's mikvah lady, called these liquids "living water." I imagined bathing in rainwater, felt drops falling in rivulets between my breasts. I inhaled deeply, knowing that the water would smell warm, clean, like steam. It was all so pure.

After a bit of sleuthing, I discovered that San Francisco and Berkeley each had a mikvah. Married women went like clockwork the specified number of days after their menses had ended. They slipped off their clothes, twisted rings from their fingers, delicately pulled wigs from their heads. Singularly, they climbed down the tiled steps and folded themselves into the warmth of the solitary bath.

I was almost ready. I waited until I was in the midst of my menstrual cycle—David wryly called it my "moon phase," and Jewish law called it "flux"—and then nervously placed a call to the San Francisco mikvah to make an appointment. I wasn't exactly sure where I was in my cycle. Had it been four, five, or six days after onset? How would I know when to immerse?

Ava, the head mikvah lady, quickly realized I was a stranger to her domain.

"Oh? You've never been to the mikvah? You're getting married, maybe? You want to come before the wedding, yes?"

"No. I'm already married." I said this quietly.

"Oh?" It was a question. "And which synagogue do you belong to?" Suspicion edged her voice.

I faltered. "Um. I don't exactly—I don't belong." I stopped, realized that I half-expected her to reject me, deny me entrance into the mikvah. I didn't have the proper intent. I was sure she could tell.

"You don't go to synagogue?"

"No. Well, a few times, actually, I've gone to services. That's it."

Silence. She cleared her throat. "Not that I should pry, but why come here now? I don't want to discourage you—all sorts of women come here. Not just the Orthodox. But the secular women, they usually come once, just before their wedding. And you? I don't understand. Tell me."

I took a breath. "It's going to sound strange. A book brought me here. I read a mystery. It was Faye Kellerman—"

Laughter ripped through the phone line. "*The Ritual Bath.* I know this book. Vay. This is crazy. You're coming to the mikvah because of a murder mystery? What can I say? You'll be the first. Vay. You're coming after your cycle, yes?"

Pause. "Yes."

Ava made a clicking sound with her tongue. "Look," she said decisively, "so you'll come. And Nadia, the attendant, will be here to help you. She'll tell you everything you need to know. You'll take off your makeup, your jewelry, your contact lenses if you wear them. You'll brush your hair, clip and clean your nails. Then Nadia will check you over, make sure you have no stray hairs, no painted nails. Nothing that isn't a living part of you—not even a piece of lint— should interrupt the connection between you and the water. When Nadia finishes looking you over, she'll lead you into the bath. There, you'll say the blessing and you'll dunk three times. One. Two. Three. Everything, even your hair, has to go under. Nadia will watch. You'll know you've done it right when you hear Nadia say, 'Kosher.'"

"*Kosher?*" I laughed.

"Yes, yes, of course. Nadia, she'll call out, 'Kosher!' so you can hear. You'll learn more when you get here. Come on Monday evening at seven—that's good for you? Don't bother with bringing a towel. We have here everything you need."

And that was that. I was in. Whether Monday was or wasn't the seventh day after my cycle ended—I was in. I scanned the wall calendar tacked to the side of my bookshelf, tried to track my way back to the first day of blood. No chance. I hadn't made a notation anywhere. I leaned against the shelves. What should I do? Should I call Ava, tell her I feared I'd be immersing before the proper number of days had passed? I resisted the urge to pick up the receiver. No. I wasn't Orthodox. I wasn't even Conservative. Why should I care?

The calendar crashed to the floor, fanned out. Damn. Religious Judaism was unnerving, an uptight hostess at an elegant party, inviting you in and then frowning when you used the wrong fork or reached too far over the table to snag a plate of food. I knew the mikvah ladies would be upset if I arrived at the bath before the traditional period of separation had ended. Besides, I was superstitious, the type who never stepped on sidewalk cracks and never walked under ladders. You could never be too careful. There was no way I'd risk bad karma by plunging into the mikvah waters while I was still spotting.

No matter where I tried to connect with Judaism, it seemed I needed an instruction manual. I searched for a metaphor. If Judaism was a map, none of the legends seemed to be of any help and my compass was a bit off-kilter. Perhaps I needed the easy-to-follow, foldout, laminated-plastic version. Or perhaps I should trash the map and follow my instincts, peering up at the sun for guidance and wetting my finger in the wind. Who knew? It was all such a mystery.

That night, when David came home, I described my conversation with Ava. I told him I'd need to dunk three times in the water.

"Here," I said, sinking to a squat, "I'll show you." I tucked my head to my chest. "Now I'm underwater. When I'm fully under—every strand of hair even—the assistant will yell, 'Kosher.' Then I know I can get up."

I stood up and squatted down again, just for emphasis. David looked at me down there, a half-smile on his face, and said, "And the attendant says, 'Kosher'?" I nodded my head.

"And then what happens?" he asked. Pause. "Is that when she brings you the pastrami sandwich?"

I found the door. It was an unpretentious dark-brown wooden thing, entirely out of place on tony Sacramento Street. But there it was, sandwiched between a furniture store and a sports shop. I passed by a Michael Jordan poster in the sports shop window, landing in front of a small black buzzer next door, where wooden letters spelled *Mikva*. I buzzed. Instantly, a middle-aged woman opened the door and smiled. She was round like a bobka. Compact. "I am Nadia," she said. Her accent was Russian.

She let me in and closed the door. We stood in a small lobby. "You are from Israel?" she said.

I was puzzled. "Israel? No, I'm from here."

"Here?" she said. She looked down at a palm-sized piece of paper, then back up at me, nodding. "Ahhh. Of course. You are woman from Oakland, yes?"

"Right. Oakland."

"You know mikvah, yes?"

My neck tightened. "No, not really. I'll need your help when I'm in the bath. I can't say the prayer."

Her brow furrowed. "You are Jewish?"

"Yes."

"You haf two Jewish parents?"

"Yes." I pushed a fallen curl out of my eye.

She peered into my face. "You are married?"

"Sure," I said loudly, "seven years." I held up my ring finger, flashed the gold.

Her eyes narrowed. "Yes, married. But why you never came before and you come now?"

Forget about bringing Faye Kellerman into this one. "Because now is the right time."

She bobbed her head, smiled. "So you will like. I am sure."

I had passed some sort of test. My neck loosened.

Nadia stepped closer to me, and for an alarming moment I thought she was going to clap me on the back. "You came here," she said excitedly, "so you can get clooseprtogadd."

Had I missed something? "What?"

"You came here," she yelled, "and you can be clooseprtogadd."

I was sure this was a critical piece of information. I tried to parse the syllables in my head. Nadia waited expectantly. I shrugged, looked up at the ceiling as though it contained answers. *Clooseprtogadd.* The syllables suddenly separated, declared themselves.

"Closer to God," I said. "I can get closer to God. Right. Of course."

"This is what I said. Yes," said Nadia, now unbelievably happy. She took a step toward the hall and motioned me to follow. "Come," she said. "We go to where you prepare."

She walked me just inside the door of the large bathroom. "You shower and clean; then ring this bell when ready."

She smiled broadly, backed out, closed the door. I was alone. I looked around. I ran my hands over the tiled wall, pulled back the shower curtain, peered into a tub so clean it gleamed. I made my way to the sink, leaned over the redwood counter to study the many ways I could clean myself. Clearly, washcloth and soap was a simple, pedestrian method, something beginners used. I fingered bottles of bleach (removed even the toughest stains from your skin), baby oil, alcohol, witch hazel, nail polish remover; I pawed through cotton balls, Q-tips, tissues, toothpicks, dental floss, nail clippers, tweezers (splinters protruding from your skin were a no-no), scissors, black plastic combs, and an assortment of brushes.

As I wiped the eyeliner from beneath my eyes, I wondered who else, how many Jews, had leaned over the sink, peered into the mirror, squeezed this particular tube of Vaseline. I stripped down, walked around the room naked, looked again at my reflection. I was too thin—bony—my skin too pale against the backdrop of blue tile. The whole scene felt antiseptic, clinical, a precursor to a thorough physical exam. Perhaps I should sit and meditate, ground myself, place my hand on my hara and follow my breath.

The showerhead was old and hung lifelessly from the wall. I stared at it, thinking. And then it occurred to me. I had been told to take a shower. I was a Jew in a tiled room. Let me make the connection clear, perfectly obvious: I flashed on other showers, German showers, other Jews—yes, millions—and for a second I saw them, crowds of skeletal women with sunken faces, crammed in a tiled room, holding hands, leaning naked skin to naked skin, bone to bone, waiting.

This is the way a mind works. It wasn't my fault. I'm not preoccupied with the Holocaust. The image arose without invitation and assaulted me. I'm a post-Holocaust Jew, and that makes my unconscious only a few degrees of separation away from images of the Holocaust. It's paradoxical, but the past rises up to the surface, even for those of us who were never there. It pollutes the present, perverts holy moments. It reminds us to remember.

I stepped into the tub, turned the shower full-on, let the force of water pelt me. Its tingling touch woke my face, shoulders, breasts, stomach, thighs. I lifted my face up to the spray, opened my mouth, tasted. I looked down at my stomach, washed the area between my legs. Was menstrual blood a form of pollution? Was I impure? I was spotting yesterday but hadn't noticed any evidence today.

After that, time passed quickly. I patted dry, wrapped myself in a towel, rang the bell for Nadia, who came in for the once-over. She didn't smile but went straight to work, a doctor examining a patient. She held my hands as she studied my nails, touched the top of my shoulder as she trapped a stray sliver of thread and pulled it gently from my hair. Then she placed a pair of paper slippers in front of my feet. "The bottoms of your feet, they should not pick up even a speck of something on the way to the mikvah," she said, motioning for me to slip into them.

Finally, I got the nod of approval. She opened the back door and led me to the mikvah. She took my towel, averting her eyes from my body, and motioned for me to enter the water. I stepped down the steps and was engulfed by warmth. I immersed once.

"You say the blessing," said Nadia, when I emerged. She pointed to the wall, where the blessing was spelled out in Hebrew. Then, for my benefit, she began voicing the blessing herself, pausing after each word so I could repeat the sounds.

"Now you go under. Everything—hair too—goes underwater. Do not touch the sides. Two more times, you do this." She looked down at me, a captain instructing her charge.

I went under and so did my hair. I went once again, curling my head into my chest and tucking my knees. Bingo. That's when I happened to brush my entire forearm cleanly against the tiled wall of the bath.

"Kosher," she yelled, and when I rose I saw that she'd squared her shoulders proudly. She hadn't noticed my transgression, and I didn't have the heart to tell her my last dunk had been moot, unkosher.

Afterwards, back in the bathroom, I leaned over the sink, peered at my face in the mirror. I ran my fingers through my wet hair, blew water out my nose. Exotic? No. Transformative? No, not this experience. I had found no answers. Instead, I framed a question: *What does it take to transform a moment into holiness?*

I went to see Ruth, a Hasidic woman from the Berkeley mikvah. She told me each of her days was holy. Every morning she unlocked the mikvah door, turned on the lights, ran her finger over the tiles before anyone else arrived. She kept the books, folded the towels, stocked the counter, witnessed women old and young as they entered the waters.

Her wig was a perfect brown bob. I watched its every move. We were at her house, a few yards away from the mikvah building. We leaned over a dining room table heaped with books, papers, and the sticky remnants of her kids to talk in between her mikvah duties.

I grilled her, asked one question after another, didn't hide my own sense of unease. Smart and interesting, she patiently provided answers for a good while. After an hour, though, I'd perhaps asked too many questions, expressed too much skepticism. She threw up her hands. "You can either believe in mikvah or not," she said finally. "If you do believe, then you say, 'This is it, the law that God gave. I can't be with my husband when I'm in the spiritual state of niddah.' And if you don't believe," she shrugged, "that's your prerogative. But mikvah is one of our commandments as Jews."

I began to tire. I shifted focus to my sleeve, which seemed to be stuck to the table. I tugged, and the sleeve resisted. I pulled again, leaned backwards.

Ruth looked at nothing but my face. "I know, in fact, that you don't believe. I can tell. But I still think you should go to the mikvah according to Jewish law, during the time after you menstruate. I say, *Go ahead, do it*. What do you have to lose? Nothing. You may surprise yourself. You may discover something you can't even envision."

Tug. Pull. Zzzzzt. My sleeve came free. My fingers grabbed the remnant of what looked like a half-sucked cough drop. The thing attached itself to my index finger and thumb. I put my hand under the table and shook wildly. Ruth began to straighten the papers in front of her.

"Let me tell you this," she said. "Before I became Orthodox, I was a microbiology student. I studied life you can't see with the naked eye. I saw how much in the world just isn't known and how much can't be explained. I realized there are questions science can't answer. I suddenly found a sense of spirit. There is a God. There is a creator who created the world. He gave us instructions. And mikvah is one of them."

Fling. Thud. The cough drop jettisoned, smacked against something hard. Just then the clock struck the hour. Bells chimed. I was ready to go. We looked at each other. Ruth led me to the door, where she took my hand.

"It can happen," she said. "You may find one day at the mikvah that you've begun to experience something that goes beyond the written page." And then, after a squeeze of my hand, she let go.

The final stop. I went to see Rabbi Jane Litman at congregation Sha'ar Zahav in San Francisco. This wouldn't be the first time I'd end up sitting across from her, firing questions in her office. But she was always unflappable, even in the face of my most critical barbs against Judaism. And she always had an answer.

Today I watched as a small cluster of congregants mobbed her when she breezed into the lobby. "Hey, Jane," yelled a nose-ringed woman, "you look great. Well rested. Much more relaxed than I've seen you in awhile."

Rabbi Litman threw up her hands. "I spent the weekend at an ashram. Steamed rice, straw mats, a vow of silence—just what I needed. You know what it's been like here this past month, right? Deaths, one after another. Very, very difficult time. So this weekend I went away, renewed myself."

She saw me and smiled, waved me over. "Come on over here. Nothing to be afraid of—well, not much anyway. Let's head to my office."

I followed her, remembering the first time we'd talked. "You can say whatever you want," she'd said, leading me toward a chair. "Judaism is a system that allows us to voice our discontent."

And now I sank into the cushions once again. "The whole idea of mikvah, for women—" I said.

"Yes?" She sat across from me.

"Frankly, it sucks."

She raised her brow. "Have you been to one?"

"Sure. Sacramento Street. It was a drag. Water went up my nose. My arm touched the side. I worried about whether I was following religious instructions in the right way."

She laughed. "That's one kind of mikvah experience. Don't worry so much about rules."

"You're kidding, aren't you? The whole practice is about rules. You scrub yourself with every imaginable cleanser. You press your feet into crunchy brown-paper slippers so they can't pick up a speck of dirt when you're shuffling from the shower to the mikvah. You ring the bell, wait while some woman practically picks lint from your navel. Nothing should separate you from the water, right?"

She leaned forward. "The Orthodox, they sometimes obsess about these things. When I'm at the mikvah, I'm not thinking about rules. I'm thinking, *Where does my body end and the outside world begin?* I experience my body as totally at one with lint, with whatever else is there. Whatever manages to get into that mikvah is my body.

"Mikvah is beautiful," she continued. "It's all about warm pure water, rainwater and stream water. It's about being quiet and alone in a pretty place with your own body. It's about liking your body. American culture teaches women to hate their bodies. Judaism teaches women to love their bodies — that whole effort to negate the body isn't a Jewish thing. And I think mikvah is a place where women's bodies are honored."

"So you do go to the mikvah?" I asked.

"I do."

"Regularly?"

"Yes."

"On the right day?"

"No. But what is the right day? I go on the right day for me."

"And that day has nothing to do with your menses?"

"Nothing. It has to do with my intention. There's an authentic, affirmed streak in Judaism, in Jewish text, that says it's fine to do things out of your *kavannah*, out of your intentionality. Intentionality is that still, small voice inside, the prophetic voice that God gave you. So my mikvah usage tends to follow intentionality. I tend not to go when I'm having my period, though I couldn't say I never have."

"Have you ever gone to the mikvah when you were still spotting?" I was still fixated on what happens when you don't follow the rules.

"Probably, though I can't think of a particular time right now."

"And you didn't feel like you were going to be cursed?"

"Cursed? No. You can't curse a mikvah. You could throw a pig in a mikvah. Mikvahs exist the other way around." She stopped, thought for a minute.

89

"Look," she said. "One is in dynamic tension with the Jewish tradition. That is to say, Judaism isn't a fundamentalist tradition. Judaism—even the most Orthodox Judaism—believes in ongoing revelation."

She leaned forward. "I think you need to do a mikvah with me. We'll do a spiritual immersion. Next week?"

I nodded. The words *ongoing revelation* rebounded in my head. Rabbi Litman checked her book. "Tuesday—late morning, say? Maybe at ten?"

"Tuesday."

It was set. I left the office and headed home.

Tuesday morning, San Francisco. I shifted the car into third. Revelations are a kind of transformation, I realized. And transformation is slow and misleading. It happens quietly, invisibly, without the crash of cymbals or the cheers of crowds. The gray areas—the exact moment when day turns to night or when an adolescent boy turns into a man—are confusing, hard to pinpoint.

Brake lights ahead. I released the clutch again and eased into second.

In human lives, transformation is synonymous with rites of passage: birth, marriage, death. It was Dutch anthropologist Arnold van Gennep and later Victor Turner who discovered and explored the idea that three stages are common to all rites of passage: separation, liminality, and reintegration.

Liminality is the gray area. It's the step before transformation, a necessary and uncomfortable state of being. It had fascinated me since I learned of it in graduate school. Turner called it the state of being betwixt and between, and wrote about it in reams. It's a phase of unease. Insecurity. Not-knowing. Ambivalence.

Here's an example. Say you wanted to convert to Judaism. You'd lived with this desire for years. You no longer believed in Jesus as the messiah, and you didn't celebrate Easter or take communion. You went to synagogue on Friday nights. You finally understood that gefilte fish was *edible*—yes, not something to fear. Walking around with a last name like McCormick—attached to the notion of Christmas, perhaps, but lighting Shabbat candles with fervor—you were just before the juncture, the opening. You needed the rabbi's blessing, which was six months away. You were on the way to becoming whatever it is you would become. In the meantime, neither Christian nor Jew, you were in a spiritual netherworld. You were *liminal*. Most likely, you were anxious as well.

These are the sorts of struggles that define you. Who you are is purely magical in origin, not to be explained, just to be examined and sometimes endured. The only sure thing is that one moment will change into the next. Our lives are points of passage from one liminal stage to another. We are forever finding ourselves betwixt and between, destined to withstand long stages of discomfort in the hopes of positive change—progress of some sort.

It occurred to me, as I pulled up at a stoplight, that for too long I had been liminal. I had been someone who could neither disclaim her Judaism nor fully claim it. And I had been hoping that, somehow, the waters would clear. I would be able to escape this place of being betwixt and between.

The car at my rear beeped loudly. I looked up. The light had already turned green. American Jews have no patience for liminal states, no patience for ambiguity. Who can blame us? Those states are painful. No one supports their existence. We live in a culture that thinks pain needs to be dulled, cured, erased.

Perhaps we're missing out, I realized. Perhaps our ambiguities are holy, not something to numb. Our sense of psychological discomfort, our emotional unease, life's excruciating gray areas—all these are holy. Revelatory. They teach us what we need to know. They make us grapple with the question of who we are.

The horn behind me beeped again. Originally, I'd gone to the mikvah to experience transformation. I'd missed the whole point. It was time to go back, this time to experience my liminality, to sit with it. I hit the gas, reached the San Francisco mikvah. The attendant, who wasn't Nadia this time, ushered me gently to the bathroom and asked me to ring the bell when I was ready. Rabbi Litman would open the door and lead me to the mikvah, she said.

I showered. As the water sprayed me, I placed my palms against the wet wall tiles, closed my eyes. In her office, Rabbi Litman had said that physical structures hold the residue of holy moments. The mikvah, she'd said, held such a residue. I suddenly understood. My holy moment, the holy moments of other Jewish women—there were millions—every single holy moment was contained there, in the tiles, in the nail clippers and sponges even, in the living waters. And when I entered those waters, every holy moment, every woman's prayers, were touching me.

I stepped out of the shower, wrapped myself in a towel, and rang the bell. Water ran down my body, dripped into small pools at my feet. Rabbi Litman opened the door as I was trying to fumble my feet into a small pair of brown-paper slippers. The paper bunched. I unbunched it with my toes, tried to jam in my feet again. One slipper slid across the tile. I felt my face redden. Determined, I trapped the end of the runaway slipper with my heel, then jammed my other foot into the opening. Riiiiiip. The sound echoed off the walls.

I looked up at Rabbi Litman for guidance. She gave me a quizzical look, one that seemed to say, *Why the heck would you worry about this?* Then her expression changed. She smiled, and it was a gift that began in her eyes. She stood in the door another moment, reading my face. She didn't lean over me. She didn't check for stray hairs, for painted nails.

We moved to the next room, stood at the edge of the mikvah. She motioned for me to remove my towel. "When you walk down these seven steps into the water, try to do it with intention, with kavannah. Think of the seven days of creation, the seven days of the week."

I slipped into the water slowly, waited a moment on each step.

When I was chest-high in water, I looked up at her. I was ready to immerse.

"I want you to think about what you need to let go," she said. "Let it go. Then I want you to welcome your future, to see it rolling toward you in waves, like water. Unfold your arms. Open your body. Feel the water on you; notice the way it embraces your feet, your thighs, your chest, your neck. Close your eyes, if you like. Take a breath. Then, when you're ready and not before, immerse once."

I looked for my future and saw nothing. I tensed. I tried again and saw my mother's face, my father's hand. I groped for David in my mind and saw his piercing blue eyes before I tucked my head to my chest and sank down. Warm water filled my ears, covered me. I was under.

Maybe, I thought, we must go under at crucial moments. We must hold our breath, go down, down, until everything familiar looks murky, filmy, suddenly unclear. Go down into liminality. Go down until we have no air, until we learn what we need to know: we are all beautiful aberrations. Our despair can birth revelation. What we know is always just beyond our reach.

Rabbi Litman was above me, a witness to the moment. An intense sadness opened in me, unfolded, dissipated. My future was here. I felt its presence and understood. Always, I thought, I would be fighting to emerge. From one body of water to the next.

THE SOUND OF GOD

i was a frog. I was a bird that squeaked. I could not, for the life of
me, sing. My vocal range spanned approximately three notes.
My voice was small, like a chicken's. Whenever I tried to sing I
stopped again almost immediately, in mid-note, embarrassed by the
weak, uneven, out-of-key trickle of sound that came from my mouth.

The whole issue came to a head on a Friday night. I tried the
Shabbat service at Chochmat Halev, a center for Jewish meditation
and learning whose name means "wisdom of the heart." I knew I'd
have to peel off my shoes, sit cross-legged on the floor, meditate on
command. By the end, I'd probably have to hold hands with
strangers.

The place was packed. A boisterous crowd spilled out the door.
Mounds of worn shoes blocked the entrance. Coats were mashed
into all kinds of places. Inside, congregants covered the floor, sitting,
squatting, and kneeling knee to knee.

I arrived just in time for the guided meditation, sat near the back.
A woman in white tapped lightly on a drum and told a story about
the Baal Shem Tov, the founder of Hasidism. Periodically, she'd
pause and ask us to check in with our bodies: we'd concentrate on
our breath, our posture, the way our weight shifted lower as our bodies relaxed. The room itself seemed to settle after awhile. The people
around me began to sway, almost imperceptibly.

Then the prayers—songs, really—began. The energy in the room
shifted. I've seen this phenomenon before. People seem to come

into a service as individuals. They're separate, distracted, disconnected even, from the people around them. Then a choreography begins. The rabbi, or the cantor, or the layperson leading the service motions to the congregation. Folks lean over, pull out their prayerbooks, flip to the proper page almost in unison. They stand up, clear their throats. They open their mouths and sing.

During the songs, a change happens. These individuals become something more. They become part of a whole, a community. They become part of a heritage, a civilization. They're connected by voice, by sound, by melody. Sometimes they become part of each other, part of whatever they call God.

I grew up in a family that denied God. When I was five and curious, my sister, stamping her foot, told me that God didn't exist. She was thirteen and both of us thought she knew everything. God was a lie, she told me, a fiction, something people a long time ago had made up.

Later that day, my father confirmed her verdict. He put his hand gently on my forehead. "My sweet, the idea of God is ridiculous," he said.

I'd inherited atheism. It wasn't a tradition I'd come by honestly, after struggling with and then rejecting notions of God. For more than thirty years, I'd lived without questioning that the world existed, that I existed, that beauty and sadness and pain existed without God. As amazing as it sounds to me now, I'd never thought to experiment. I'd never decided to live—for a week or a day or a moment even—as though God just might exist.

The man on my left leaned back then forward, lost in song. His voice was sweet, like a young boy's. On my right a woman held a sheaf of prayers to her chest as she sang. Her face was flushed, her voice throaty.

I tried. I really did. Every few minutes I'd screw up my courage to sing, only to stop, moments later, when I became aware of the sound of my voice. It came from inside me, from my most private place, and it was flawed. It was ugly. It was sour, like milk gone bad. It was me. I closed my mouth.

After the service ended, as I was rising to leave, the man next to me began talking. "The singing was really beautiful, you know?"

I nodded.

"The songs are what always brings me back," he said. "They touch me. They always have, even when I didn't know what they were all about.

"I guess you could say," he continued, shrugging his shoulders and talking more to himself than to me, "that they make me feel connected to God."

As I left the building, a small knot blocked my throat. Voice. Melody. Song. Each held answers. Answers about a deeper part of myself, about the essence of Judaism, about being human—and perhaps even about something called God.

I can't escape my New York roots. When I'm low they rise up within me, yelling their wisdom. This time was no different. I was blue, a bit listless and unmoored for a week after the synagogue incident. At home, I realized that the only thing I couldn't do in front of David, after all these years, was sing. In the privacy of my car one day I took the plunge. I shut the windows, turned the radio up full volume, opened my mouth, tried to belt out a Van Morrison tune. No go. Midstream I heard myself, became conscious of my lousy voice, and shut down. I sat there, gripping the steering wheel, in a funk. That's when the voice of New York came to me. *When in doubt*, it said, *hire someone.*

Anna. This woman was a professional. Her flyer, which had the words *Life is short: Don't take it too seriously* on the cover, described her as a voice and bodywork therapist. She did something called rhythm and flow work, along with sounding, healing, holistic drumming, and tantra. I had plucked the flyer from a bulletin board at the Transformative Body massage school, a place where people go with the hope of merging their spiritual and physical bodies—in the nude, usually, and surrounded by others. Their practitioners have excellent, if far-out, reputations. Anna had spent seven years as a bodyworker at the well-known Esalen retreat, eight years studying African drumming with a Ghanaian master, and eight years teaching voice and movement classes in the Bay Area. Could I trust her with my own voice?

I tracked down the head of the Transformative Body school. Waving the flyer, I said, "Hey—will you vouch for this woman?"

He looked up from his desk. Nodding, he stubbed out the end of a clove cigarette. "She's a standout," he said, as a thin stream of smoke began to rise from somewhere in the middle of his desktop. "Trust me."

I took home the flyer. I kept rereading the copy, which mentioned breath, healing energy, and something called our primitive voices. Each time I'd finish reading the flyer, I'd toss it into the trash next to my desk. *Nope,* I'd think, *it's not for me.* Then a few hours later I'd walk back to the trash from wherever I was, sheepishly thrust in my arm, and retrieve it.

I finally called to make an appointment and soon enough found myself at her door. A tall, thin, graceful woman met me, introducing herself as Anna. She guided me inside her house, past congo drums and giant gourds, past a single whale vertebra so large I mistook it for a coffee table, past sunflowers that had dropped yellow dust in the shape of a perfect circle on the floor.

In the massage room, under the poster of Buddha, I stepped out of my clothes. When Anna turned to me and began to talk, I fervently wished I'd left on my clothes for a few moments longer. I tried to make it to the massage table with some semblance of grace but managed to bang into it before mounting.

She slipped a long silk scarf over my body. "I usually say a short prayer before I begin the session," she said. Her accent, I realized with a start, was German.

I felt her fingertips on my back. "Shall I say the prayer out loud or to myself?" she asked.

Oh no, I thought, *not a prayer.* I ticked off the possibilities: she'll invoke goddess energy, call upon spirit animals, or make an appeal to the universe.

"Out loud," I said. I wanted to hear it.

She began her prayer. "I pray that this body I'm about to touch has the wisdom to find what it needs. And I pray that I have the wisdom to step aside and allow it to happen." Her voice was melodious, as gentle as her touch. My breath deepened. My shoulders lowered.

Then she cut to the chase. "Every time you breathe," she said, pressing down on my feet, "I want you to let out a sound."

My chest tightened. "I don't breathe all that often," I said. "Bad allergies."

Her hands leaned into the backs of my calves. "Right," she said, laughing. "Look, all I ask of you is to exhale so that I can hear it," she said. "You'd be surprised at what can happen. Your breath is powerful. It gets things moving—energy, spirit, sound—it all begins to open."

She exhaled, ending with an ahhhhhh.

"Try it," she said. "Let out your song."

Silence.

"Go ahead," she urged. "Entertain yourself. Experiment. Play with the tones, pitch, and loudness of your voice."

My hands were ice-cold. My voice, like a pill caught in my throat, was stuck. Finally, a few sounds—nothing more than groans, really—escaped with my exhalations.

"Good," she said. "I heard that. Now keep going, keep breathing, keep making your sounds."

She let loose. Her own sounds were a form of enlightenment, or perhaps a kind of zoo. Trills, warbles, low moans, quivering growls came from the center of her body, from a place my voice had never been. I thought of a dog's growl, a crow's caw, a hyena's laugh. The effect was at once beautiful and unnerving. It was, I thought, a little bit insane.

"No way," I said, shifting my weight on the table. "Can't do it."

She bent over me, her palm on my forehead. "You should experience your entire range," she said.

I was startled. Voice had just become a metaphor for self-expression. When was the last time I'd played with the range of who I am? I concentrated, breathed in and out through my mouth, then reached for the breath in my gut. My voice escaped quietly, then unfolded together with Anna's, becoming louder, higher. Soon she took off alone, an infusion of sounds. She was a wind instrument, then a single plucked string.

She took her hands from my body but continued to make sounds. A strange thing happened next. My body moved as though there were small waves within me. Every sound she made invoked from me a physical response. It was as though my body was no longer connected to my brain. It was connected to her voice. We cycled through this odd, spontaneous call and response, with each of her sounds piercing me, then traveling like a ripple of water up and down my back, my neck, my arms, and my legs, making them undulate. Nothing existed for me outside of this moment. I was fully present.

Years earlier, a young Lubavitch man in Crown Heights had introduced me to *niggunim*, prayers sung without words. It was impossible to tell me about this, he said at first; it was something I had to experience. He pointed to my video camera and invited me to tape him. With the glare of lights on him and the camera a silent judge, he closed his eyes, opened his mouth, and sang. It was the sound of an ancient terrain, of escape from the everyday world. Words would have been an afterthought.

I realized then that voice has the power to enter your body. It connects you to yourself. It transports you to the intuitive world, to the divine.

After the session with Anna ended, she tried to tell me what my body movements had looked like from her vantage point above the table. She frowned, said she couldn't think of the English equivalent, and spoke a word or two in German. I stared at her blankly.

"Primal," she said suddenly, snapping her fingers. She swirled her arms in the air like snakes. "Your movements, they were reptilian," she said. She was beaming. I wondered if I should be pleased. Was this a compliment? I looked up at her, confused.

"You were in a state of grace," she said, nodding her head in affirmation.

Right. I'd just had an ecstatic experience. Either that, or I was going nuts.

Months passed. I saw Anna a few more times. She always began with the same prayer. Although my voice hadn't yet found its range, each session ended with the feeling that I'd just had a religious experience. Had I? A kabbalist, a Jewish mystic, might say I was receiving divine knowledge.

Rabbi David Cooper, in *God Is a Verb*, talks about *tzippiyah*. The word was used by a twelfth-century mystic called Isaac the Blind to describe mystical awareness, the state we experience when the sense of past and future dissolves and we're totally in the moment. Cooper says that tzippiyah, when we ponder it, can lure us into a new way of relating to the universe.

Anna. She had brought me to a place where the past and future could dissolve into the present. She had touched me both physically and with her sounds. Through her, my body and my voice were becoming connected to my spirit. I began to believe that Anna could be my conduit to a momentary experience of God.

Artists—singers, dancers, painters—have always known these momentary experiences. Take the painter. All concentration might be focused, for example, on the act of dipping the brush into a palette and sliding it over the canvas. An hour of such concentration passes and then, suddenly, the act becomes easy. A light enters the painter. For a moment, he actually feels that he's part of something larger than himself. Rembrandt spoke about these moments as times when he could feel a divine spark. He often painted ordinary people with an extraordinary light emanating from within them. Everyone, he said—every single person—has such a spark.

I went back to Anna.

In the massage room, as I took off my clothes, Anna began telling me about a disappointment. While she talked, I climbed onto the table, rolled onto my stomach, let my legs grow heavy. I lifted my neck, tilted my head upward to make eye contact with her. She was talking about Ben, a man with whom she'd been falling in love. She'd spoken about him before.

Her face was troubled. "It's over," she said. "Last night he told me he's committed to right breeding, to building a community of the right kind of people."

"Right breeding?" My stomach tightened. "He's obviously not Jewish."

"No," she said with an exhausted sigh, "he's not." She looked at me. "Are you?"

I nodded my head yes. "Didn't you know?" *Does it show?*

"I wasn't certain," she said.

"Yup," I said. "So just those two short words—right breeding—make me tense. I think of Hitler."

We stared at each other. "Exactly," she said.

She stepped back from me. "I want to tell you something about my past," she said. "I spent my whole childhood in a household of silence. I was born in Germany just after the Holocaust ended. It was a country of destruction and devastation. It had no soul. No one I knew spoke of the Holocaust, yet it was there. It was everywhere. You couldn't get away from it. I wanted to know what had happened, what really had happened, but no one would tell me. At home, I learned that I wasn't to ask questions.

"I grew up in a house of secrets," she continued. "It wasn't until I was a teenager that I learned the truth about my father." She leaned forward. "He was a Nazi officer during the Holocaust. High up. Powerful. After the war ended he was sent to prison in another country as a war criminal. I was born sometime after he was released.

"My parents always seemed worried, haunted. I could only guess at why. Were they afraid other secrets would be uncovered? Always, there were whisperings I wasn't a part of. Always, I wondered what, exactly, he had done. And had my mother taken part? In any way at all?"

Her eyes became wet. "They were my parents, and I loved them. My father hadn't killed anyone. How could he? How could he be evil?" She stopped, looked at me. She was waiting for an answer.

The question assaulted me: How could anyone—Nazis, ordinary Germans even—have participated in the systematic torture and slaughter of six million people? Daniel Jonah Goldhagen, in *Hitler's Willing Executioners: Ordinary Germans and the Holocaust*, tried to answer that question. Early on in the book, he asked readers to imagine, just as an exercise, changing places with those Germans, performing their deeds, acting as they had. To do this exercise, he said, ". . . we must always bear in mind the essential nature of their actions as perpetrators: they were killing defenseless men, women, and children, people who were obviously of no martial threat to them, often emaciated and weak, in unmistakable physical and emotional agony, and sometimes begging for their lives or those of their children."

Yet these were ordinary men. Mornings, they shot Jews for sport, as though picking off rabbits in a hunting game. They held children by their legs and spun them round, smashing their small heads into brick walls. They made people dig their own graves. They turned the word *shower* into something unspeakable. Evenings, they went home, kissed their wives, drank their beers, tucked their daughters into bed.

"Your father killed people," I said. "That was his job, and that's what he believed was right. He was purifying Germany. You want to know how he could kill Jews? He believed that we were less than human. We were subhuman. We were animals." I said this as though I were reporting the weather. *The temperature will be fifty degrees today. Winds from the east.* Where were my emotions?

I have touched someone who has touched a Nazi. Her palms, which have cradled my head, smoothed oil down my spine, been offered in pleasure, have been held by hands that kept a crematorium running. Or signed death orders. Her voice, which has merged with mine, entered me, has said *I love you* to a Nazi. We have shared not only touch and voice, things we could feel and hear, but molecules, atoms, energy too, the essential elements of ourselves.

I wasn't sure what to do, so I did nothing. Anna was still speaking—telling me the story of her parents, which was the story of herself and of a particular time in Germany—but I was only half-listening.

A tape was running in my head. I heard my father telling story after story of relatives, those who'd died in the Holocaust, those who'd survived Auschwitz and Dachau. Now he was describing the time his cousin Moses had looked up from the fields outside Cracow and seen smoke rising from the city. Moses had known at once that the Nazis were setting Jewish homes aflame. He hadn't yet known that the soldiers had first prodded families out of each house and shot them. It wasn't until he arrived home, breathless, that he saw his house burned, saw his family dead—his young wife, his two sons fallen side by side.

I was still naked. Anna seemed not to notice. My back was getting cold. My breasts were crushed against the table. I pushed myself up onto my elbows. Why didn't I sit up, get off the table, and get dressed? Get the hell out of there? I was afraid she'd stop talking. Stop telling. The moment was delicately balanced. I was receiving a kind of confession. Did Anna want absolution? The whole scene could have been classified as alternative therapy: *Trained nude female listener wants to hear your painful life story. See her nakedness as a metaphor for your own vulnerability. Bare your soul. Nonjudgment is our specialty. Call for appointment.*

The air was charged. "Maybe everyone — each of us — has a capacity for cruelty," I said. It sounded bland, half-hearted, even to me.

Silence. We looked toward the clock and realized, with surprise, that more than an hour had passed. I wasn't going to be getting voice- or bodywork today.

I had committed an enormous, undefined act of cultural disloyalty. The spirits of my cousins, my aunts, and my uncles would come back from the dead. They would visit me at night, their eyes large with dismay.

A sudden thought consumed me: *Anna, too, has suffered because of the Holocaust.* This thought was somehow one too many. I didn't want to examine its implications. I wanted to leave. I got up, finally. Got dressed. She hugged me, thanked me. She looked into my eyes, paused, and thanked me once again for listening.

"Of course I listened," I said, smiling tightly, still in her embrace. "What else could I do? You had me there, trapped in the room, waiting for my treatment." Something was wrong. I didn't sound like I was teasing.

I know why we tell stories. They consecrate moments, illuminate the dark. They make sense of our random lives. They teach us things we may never understand.

Anna and I looked at each other, uncertain, then broke the hug. I said goodbye to the woman I'd once thought could lead me to God. Then I left.

I couldn't go back. Something intangible had become perverted. Something that had been right now felt wrong. The few times I'd tried to call and make another appointment, my gut had resisted. Uncomfortable, I'd placed the receiver back in its base without dialing.

THE SOUND OF GOD

For weeks, I floundered. I went on long hikes in the hills. I ate unsalted pretzels by the bagful and stared out the window. I sank into the couch, slipped my headphones on, cranked the volume and wanted only rock—the harshness of Alanis Morissette, the discordance of Smashing Pumpkins.

Then I stumbled onto the music of Andy Statman. The CD was called *Between Heaven and Earth: Music of the Jewish Mystics*. If John Coltrane had been an Orthodox Jew, his music would have sounded like Statman's. I lowered the volume and began to listen with intensity, as though I could find answers in the melodies.

It was a CD of *niggunim*, the melodic prayers without words I'd first heard in Crown Heights years ago. Statman, a master of klezmer, had taken this traditional Hasidic music and carefully woven in threads of jazz, bluegrass, and other traditions. The music moved through many states of consciousness. It was clear that Statman knew something about the life of the sacred. I called him.

He explained that niggunim were set up to induce spiritual experiences. "They were written by *tzaddikim*, saints, who are on very high spiritual levels. These tzaddikim understood not only the power of melody, but the power of going from one note to another. They knew what the emotional and spiritual essence of the particular musical interval would be, and constructed these niggunim to uplift people, to bring them closer to God. So this music is one way of approaching God."

I wanted to know what it was like to approach God. "Is music the way you, personally, reach God?" I asked.

"Music is a path, yes, but keep in mind that this music is coming out of an experience of living life according to *halakah*, according to Jewish law. The melodies were written by people who lived a whole life according to Torah. So the melodies bespeak that experience."

He kept returning to the idea of following Jewish law. As an Orthodox Jew, his life was committed to following the Torah and performing *mitzvot*, or commandments. He said that this was God's blueprint for creation.

"Jews are on a mission from God, as crazy as that sounds. I don't mean this in an evangelical way. It's just that if you believe the Torah, you believe that Jews are to be 'a light unto the nations.' Our job is to follow the Torah and observe the mitzvot. In doing this, we become close to God. And then, in this closeness, we can lift up and repair the nations of the world. That's why we're here."

I couldn't repair the world. And I knew I didn't have it in me to keep kosher, to say blessings, to do any one of the hundreds of mitzvot that Orthodox Jews followed as a rule. I steered Statman back to his music.

"The music I'm playing now is amazing," he said. "After the band finishes, the audience is elated. People—secular folks—have told us they've seen angels. After a set ends I've had experiences of hearing every sound as music, from water dripping out of a faucet to cars moving down the street. It's incredible."

He paused. "The music is a way of experiencing God's goodness and having an experience of God. Maybe you can say this kind of experience is what we mean by knowing God. I'm not quite sure exactly—I'm no prophet. I'm just a musician, trying in my own poor way to explain the little bit that I might know."

I felt close to discovery. "Have you developed your own concept of God?" I asked.

He balked. "No," he said. "The human mind can't understand what God is. It's beyond us. It's impossible for us to know God. It would be like looking at the sun; you'd go blind. You can't know what God is, but God allows us to relate to him through certain means and ways. The way to know God is to fulfill his will, and God's will for a Jew is to go to the Torah and follow the mitzvot. That's our path."

I needed another way to God. I respected Statman's wisdom but couldn't follow his lead. Mitzvot, halakah—these weren't for me.

What, then? I turned to social anthropology. Social anthropology looks at people, at who we are in relation to society, at what we believe and how we practice. I checked back over my old notes, poked around in my bookshelves. I discovered that most of the theorists—the sociologists who looked at the elementary forms of religion and the anthropologists who followed in their theoretical tracks—had not believed in God.

There were the Victorian-era theorists—Spencer, Tyler, Durkheim—who said that everything we do fulfills a social need. We weep, said Durkheim, answering the question of why people cry at funerals, not just because we're sad but because society forces us to. We believe in God because society tells us to. Our belief in God, he said, is part of a complex system that keeps people in order.

There was anthropologist Lévi-Strauss, founder of structuralism, who said our beliefs were manifestations of universal patterns in the human mind. No matter where we came from—whether we were Dayaks in Borneo or Nuer in the southern Sudan or Jews in Oakland—our brains had the same internal structures. They worked in the same way. Our belief in God, then, was a reflection of the way our brains were wired.

Something was wrong. I paged through my notebooks. These men, they left out the spiritual; they explained it away. They had a cerebral disdain for the divine. I changed gears. I looked elsewhere for wisdom.

Jewish philosopher Martin Buber said that if each of us met other people and the world with our whole being, holding nothing back, we would eventually sense and hear God. Buber's God entered into a relationship with every person on earth. The flaw with his God, in my view, was that in times of tragedy and evil, like the Holocaust, God somehow stepped out. Buber used the phrase "the eclipse of God" to describe the times when God wasn't available. As humans, we were supposed to wait, our mouths opening and closing like baby birds. We were supposed to have faith that eventually God would return.

I wanted an explanation that made room for the human capacity for evil. The mystics gave me answers. Rabbi David Cooper said that the *Zohar*, one of the most important of the kabbalistic texts, explains that within evil is the spark of goodness, and within goodness is the spark of evil. Nothing is all good; nothing is all evil. Everything contains its opposite.

Divine sparks. They were the emanations that Rembrandt had tried to capture with his brush. They were the musical journeys of Andy Statman. They were, perhaps, the touch and sounds of Anna.

In *A History of God*, scholar Karen Armstrong said that throughout the ages, mystics have counseled people to create a sense of God for themselves. Whether Jewish, Christian, or Islamic, mystics have always approached God through music, dance, sculpture, and stories; through art and imagination. According to Armstrong, imagination is our chief religious faculty, the way for each of us to conceive of God.

It was time. I would go to the border of things, to the place inside myself where art originated. I would go to my center, where language equaled silence, where bodies breathed and tongues could taste the air. I would create my own definition of God. It was time to experiment, to live for a moment as though God just might exist.

I went back to Anna. This time, I kept on my clothes.

"Before we start," I said, "can I ask you something?"

Anna nodded. She was sitting cross-legged on a large Persian floor cushion in the center of the room. I faced her. When I'd first arrived, she hadn't asked me why I'd stayed away so long. Instead, she'd opened the front door, leaned over, and embraced me.

"I've been thinking about you," I said now, "and about our last session together. You told me you came from a country of destruction. Of devastation. Of death. You grew up in Germany, you said, in a particular household with a particular history, and you were surrounded by the aftermath of horror." Suddenly unsure of myself, I looked up at her. Again, she nodded for me to continue.

"I've been wondering. Were you able to believe in God? Do you believe in God now? And if you do, then how do you explain—to yourself—a God that can permit the dark, evil side of life? A God that can allow the Holocaust?"

She stared at me, motionless. Finally, she took a deep breath. "I don't use the word *God* or believe that there's an almighty Being up there." She pointed toward the ceiling. "The word I use is *spirit*. I think spirit is everywhere. It's inside of us. I can feel it, and—you know me—I need to physically feel things. I work from the body. The body holds everything, even the soul. And our souls, they manifest in art. Look at all the incredible things we create," she said, her hands moving as though shaping the air. "We create paintings, sculptures. We do theater, dance. We write; we sing. This—all of this—is our soul in action."

"I heard someone say recently that voice is a vehicle to God," I said.

"Yes, of course," she agreed, her own voice rising in excitement. "But it's not only the voice that connects you to God. It's music. All kinds of music. Our music—the music of our bodies. We are, each of us, beautiful music. And I'm not talking about this on a spiritual level now. Physiologically, we're made up of rhythms, systems of impeccable timing. Think of the way our blood circulates, the way our bodies breathe, digest food, transform—think of all this as the music happening inside this body." She tapped on her chest for emphasis. "There's a symphony inside."

She leaned further toward me. "And what else is inside of us? Darkness. When we don't face our own dark sides, perhaps they manifest outside of us. As evil. As the Holocaust. If we have other vehicles, the darkness can come out in painting, in theater. I believe that we each must confront our own darkness somehow. Mine has to do with Germany."

We sat in silence for a moment. "Enough?" she asked gently. "Good. Now let's play."

I stretched out on the rug, with my hands on my stomach, as Anna directed. "First, we breathe," she said. Within minutes, my head was light from taking in too many breaths too fast. My throat closed. I was back to where I'd started.

I lifted my head. "This isn't going to work," I said.

"Just breathe," she said, inhaling. "Don't think about your voice just yet." She exhaled loudly.

We breathed together for a little while. I closed my eyes.

"Now," Anna said, "we're going to play with our voices. Just follow mine." Her voice started out as a whisper, moved to the back of her throat in a guttural cough, lurched up an octave, shrieked, then ended in gargles.

My voice was stuck.

She stopped. "Still you're resisting," she said. "What is it? Can you tell me? What goes on in your head?"

I turned on my side. I twisted a loose button on my shirt. "What if you think I have a bad voice, or I'm off-key, out of tune?"

She looked at me, uncomprehending. Her brow was furrowed.

"I'm afraid that once you really hear me, you'll think I have a lousy voice."

"Why?" she asked, confused.

"Because I have a lousy voice."

"That's not possible," she said, shaking her head. "There are no bad voices. There are no ugly voices, no out-of-tune ones—not to my ears, anyway." She touched my shoulder with her finger. "All voices are beautiful. You can make any sound in the world. Any sound that comes from you will be full of life. It will be your music. So get that thought out of your head and out of this room."

Something shifted within me.

"We're meant to make sounds," Anna said. She took my hand, turned it palm in, and led it to the center of my chest. "There," she said. "Now try to imitate my sounds."

"Haahaahaahaa," she said, drawing out the sound. I mimicked her, and to my surprise felt a rumble just beneath my palm.

"Do you feel the vibration? Now put your hand gently against your throat. Yes," she said, watching me. "I want you to feel that. That's your vibration. That's you, my friend."

I could feel my voice. Each sound had shape, weight, texture. I sang. I bellowed. I moved my palm to my stomach, to the top of my head. It was early evening. It was the first of May. It was the beginning of something.

These are the moments for which we wait. They come upon us from behind, move as quickly as water. I think of them as gifts.

I'm amazed by life. Amazed at our journeys, our entanglements, our tenacity in reaching out. We reach out. We keep reaching out. I thought of Buber. *If each of us meets other people and the world with our whole being, holding nothing back, we will sense God.*

The session ended. "You're ready to work now without me," Anna said.

"Without you?"

"Yes." She began to pick up the pillows. "You don't need me. Trust this. Go ahead. Find your range. Make your music."

"Without you?"

She stood there, one large pillow under each arm, and smiled.

I ended up at congregation Sha'ar Zahav in San Francisco, Rabbi Litman's synagogue. The congregation offered niggunim services twice a month. I'd heard that these services were short, quite beautiful, and open to all comers. I arrived early, sat down, waited for the others to show up.

About ten other Jews came. We sat two or three to a pew, with dozens of empty rows behind us. We weren't a large force. I didn't expect we'd have a large voice.

Two women, Jhos and her life-partner, Bon, led the service. They sat up front, facing the rest of us. Jhos, straightening her prayer shawl, got right to the point. "We'll sing for about fifteen minutes; then we'll be silent for awhile; then we'll sing again. These niggunim, these chants, they'll open you up. You'll see."

She looked at Bon. Bon closed her eyes, leaned back in her chair, and began to sing two lines over and over. The sound was eerie, haunting. It was old Jerusalem. It was a bearded old Hasidic man in a crumbling synagogue. It was a trail that I began to follow.

I joined in. I listened to my own voice. At first it was weak and sounded wrong. When the woman one pew ahead of me turned around I fell silent, thinking my voice had somehow thrown her off. Not the case. A moment later I realized she hadn't been looking at me at all, but instead had simply turned to stretch her neck.

I began again. The tune caught me. I became interested in my voice, in how loud I could be, or how long I could hold a note. I noticed the roundness of it, heard when my voice began in my stomach and rose up, rather than starting somewhere in the back of my mouth. I sang high. I sang low. I breathed through some notes, held my breath for others. All I could hear was myself.

After a time, Jhos gave the signal and we softened to a close. Silence. For a minute I heard nothing. I noticed the inside of my head, the way it was pulsating. Then I found myself listening to the room. It was silent. Or was it? The emptiness was filling in bit by bit. I heard the creak of wood. The *shush* of clothes against a pew. From outside, a motor kicked in. A bus hissed. A woman shouted in Spanish.

There is no silence. It is all inhabited. It is dense with sound.

This is the sound of God. It will come at dawn, or at the first scattered signs of night. It will reveal itself in your body, true as an electric current. It will intoxicate you. It will be a point of punctuation; the beginning, middle, and end of an impossible narrative. It will be as fluid as yourself, forming and reforming, being born and then being born again.

Outside, the sky was dark. Outside, people were passing by the door of the synagogue. I began to hear their voices, each of them. In front of me, Jhos nodded and a new chant began. In front of me, a slender woman sang and her voice was a rose. Behind me, a large man sang—and his voice, it stretched the length of the city, it streaked the sky.

There, in the synagogue, I chanted. My voice raised with the rest. We were—each of us—lamps, inexplicably lit from within.

THE KABBALISTS

I t was long after midnight in the city. It was a night of strangers and labyrinthine conversations and drinks so clear that the green light of the bar's Tiffany lamps shone through them. It was a night when my eyesight blurred briefly and a vase seemed to sway of its own accord. It was a night when I watched as a drunk, bearded man on the barstool next to me flattened a matchbook with the back of his sweaty hand and scrawled these words across it: *Shatter the physical world.*

What is it about the city in the dark hours just before dawn? At 2 A.M. the city is a different creature. It's a place of unpredictable rhythms, prophetic voices, turbulent embraces. The best way to travel through it is unhurriedly but with awareness. Every instant can offer you choices.

At 2 A.M. you can choose whether or not to notice that the night opens before you in layers as thin and translucent as insect wings. You can choose whether or not to ignore the words of the bedraggled woman on the corner who crosses herself, then shouts at the stars. You can decide to believe that whatever is happening in front of you is happenstance. You can shrug it off as nothing more than coincidence. Or you can see it as a sign.

Shatter the physical world.

It was at 2 A.M. that the guy gave me the matchbook. The unceremonious moment went something like this. He stood up, dropped the flimsy bit of cardboard into my lap, and tottered off the barstool.

He leaned precariously to the left, then to the right, stepped forward several times uncertainly, and then, gathering momentum, hurled his body through the open door, vanishing into the night.

Who wouldn't view that as a sign? I reached for my backpack, rummaged through for the book I'd been reading earlier in the day, a worn translation of the *Sefer Yetzirah* (The Book of Creation). It spoke of sacred paths and gates, magical powers and qualities, divine emanations and sacred consciousnesses. It spoke of secret names and numbers, of the relationship between energy, matter, and space. It said that angels existed and differed from men. It said that breath was the seat of consciousness. It promised that chanting had power, that God could be experienced, that language could reveal a hidden world.

This was part of kabbalah, the esoteric tradition of Jewish mystical teachings. The book itself, a remnant from either the third, fourth, fifth, or sixth century (depending upon which scholar you believe), repeatedly distorted the limits of rational thought. According to kabbalah scholar Gershom Scholem, *Sefer Yetzirah* was written in Palestine by a devout Jew with mystical leanings. As one of the first kabbalistic texts, *Sefer Yetzirah* proved to be important to the early development of kabbalah. To me, however, it seemed a disjointed collection of bizarre wisdom and magic—black and white.

Want to animate an inanimate object? Need advice on how to do it?

According to *Sefer Yetzirah*, you'd need total and utter concentration, along with specific ingredients. Suppose you wanted to create a golem, for example—a clay figure brought to life. You'd need to find a special field, bend down, dig shovelfuls of virgin soil, and gather pure spring water directly from the earth. (Water that's been placed in any kind of vessel can't be used.) You'd have to wear white vestments, work diligently to knead soil and water. Then you'd need to do specific breathing exercises and chant the letters of God's name in Hebrew—*yud heh vav heh*—together with an array of 221 pairs of the twenty-two Hebrew letters. If you did this step properly—taking a single breath between each letter, sitting with your face toward the east, moving your head slowly and deliberately with each exhalation—you'd finish the chanting sequence in just over thirty-five hours.

And if you'd gotten this far—well, were you a wacko? Who's to say? Rabbi Dov Baer, the great eighteenth-century Hasidic master, the Maggid of Mezritch, said that when a person contemplates a physical object completely and totally, he can actually transform it, first to nothingness, then to whatever he desires. Anyone using such powers of concentration would be in a nonnormative state, of course, free from the mental static that normally fills the human brain. He'd be high up on the ladder of spiritual and mystical development. And he'd understand that this exercise was dangerous, not something to be attempted alone.

The word *kabbalah* literally means "to receive." In his book *Kabbalah*, Scholem noted the impossibility of trying to define kabbalah as a single system of practice or belief. Perhaps kabbalah was like Judaism itself, a tradition with many approaches—some of which were widely separated from one another—but having in common particular unshakable symbols and ideas.

What were the ideas common to kabbalah? Scholem referred to *tendencies* and said that there were two: one mystical, one speculative. He said that the mystical tendency was expressed in images and symbols—things like charts of divine emanations, maps of the zodiac. The speculative tendency gave ideational meaning to these symbols, offered speculation as a kind of philosophy. The result? From my vantage point, conceptual confusion.

From the back of the bar I heard the clink of two glasses. I looked down at the book open in front of me. *Sefer Yetzirah* attempted nothing short of showing that all things seen and unseen were somehow connected in the universe. There were thirty-two mystical paths of wisdom, for example. Thirty-one of these paths paralleled the thirty-one nerves that emanated from the human spinal cord. The thirty-second path corresponded to the entire complex of cranial nerves, which (the book pointed out) numbered twelve. Significant? Yes—wasn't everything?

There were seven days of the week, which paralleled seven planets (Saturn, Jupiter, Mars, Sun, Venus, Mercury, and Moon), which in turn mapped to seven angels (Kaptziel, Tzidkiel, Samael, Raphael, Anathiel, Michael, and Gabriel), seven attributes (independence, wealth, intellect, dependence, inaction, generosity, blood), and seven body parts (best left here to the imagination).

In the dim light of the bar, I flipped through the pages. I skimmed over dozens of diagrams—circles and squares, triangles, pentagrams, hexagrams, as well as pages with columns of numbers. I even puzzled through a sketch of the force that counteracts the electromagnetic repulsion of a particle of matter.

I fingered the lip of the shot glass in front of me. I picked up a lime wedge, licked the sides of it absentmindedly. The tartness puckered my mouth, furrowed my brow. East. West. North. South. Four directions. Four camps in the ancient desert. Twelve diagonal boundaries and twelve permutations of the name of God. These complex and repeated maps of relationships—what were they? Obfuscations?

It occurred to me: perhaps they were rays of light. Perhaps they showed a structure under the surface. My spinal nerves could link to paths of sacred wisdom. A day as mundane as Monday could map to the heavens. Every single thing in the physical world had a hidden dimension. Over and over, the kabbalists were saying that the reality seen through my eyes isn't the only one.

Shatter the physical world.

I remembered a recent conversation I'd had with Rodger Kamenetz, who'd spent a good while studying some of the hidden aspects of Judaism. I'd read his latest book, *Stalking Elijah: Adventures with Today's Jewish Mystical Masters*, which chronicled his search.

"Why so many lists and charts and diagrams in the kabbalah?" I'd asked on the phone. It was the first time we'd spoken since the previous year, when he'd talked with me about Jewish Buddhists. "Why so much emphasis on numerology, on how numbers relate to letters, on the constellations and how the cosmos relates to the human body?"

"We need maps," he said. "As we're going through life stumbling around, we're confused, we're looking for maps that will tell us, *Ahhh, here's where I am and here's how I can get to this next place.* I think what Reb Zalman Schachter-Shalomi has been doing is brilliant. It comes from Hasidism. What he does is to psychologize kabbalah, to see kabbalah as a system that provides a map of who we are inside. Reb Zalman talks about the elements of kabbalah as reality maps. These reality maps have tremendous value because they force us to look at a larger picture. They show us that there are different realms of experience."

"So the kabbalistic attention to the significance of numbers— that's a reality map?" I asked.

"The numerology—yes. You could say it provided stepping stones for some of those mystical geniuses to make connections. In Hebrew, every letter is also a number—they didn't have Arabic numerals back then—so quite naturally, those folks who studied the texts looked at a page one way and saw it as a page of letters, then looked at it another way and saw it as a page of numbers. And after awhile they started to make equivalencies. They might have said, for example, 'Oh, I see that twenty-six showed up here and showed up there, so let's figure out if the two things are connected.'"

Reality maps. Kamenetz had offered me a tool, something that might crack open the text. "I've been so puzzled by all this stuff," I said. "It's been a fog of confusion."

"I think it's quite natural, what you're going through," he said reassuringly. "You need to find things out as an individual because that's where you start, but at a certain point you need to find a community, like-minded people who can take you to the next level."

"A community?"

"Yes. The *Sefer Yetzirah*, the *Zohar*, the Talmud too—these aren't texts you can just sit down with and read alone. The Jewish textual tradition, it just doesn't work that way. It's really designed to be studied with a partner and to be taken in slowly and to be argued back and forth."

What he described was the exact opposite of my approach. "I've been trying to pick up the *Sefer Yetzirah* at odd times of the day and read it alone."

"You can't. And this gets back to the whole notion of community that we touched on last year. In a funny way, the whole Jewish textual trip is designed to create community. If you go back to traditional Judaism, you'll find that people, when they studied the Talmud, studied it with a partner. The relationship with your study partner was intimate and profound and lived."

He paused, then began again. "And you know what? That was just the context for normative Judaism. Think of the mystical tradition—where this communal commitment was even more important. These were people who were a minority within a minority. They were a small, intimate group of people—those who formed holy communities. There's an interesting document in Jerusalem showing that there was a particular group of Jews—mystics—who pledged together to help each other's souls in this lifetime and the next. This reflects the idea that when you're studying text, you're doing it to improve yourself and help others."

The bartender's shout interrupted my thoughts. "Last call! Order it up now, people!"

I ordered one last shot of tequila and gulped it down. I felt pleasantly fuzzy. Not exactly drunk, but close. I imagined pushing myself over the edge, altering my consciousness. Didn't mystics have a tradition of imbibing?

At a certain point you need to find a community, like-minded people to take you to the next level. Kamenetz's words rebounded in my head.

As far back as I can remember, I've been most comfortable alone, where I can disappear into my own odd progression of thoughts, follow the scattered images in my mind. When I'm in the midst of a group of people I often imagine myself alone still. I can easily vanish, soar on thoughts of my own making, leave my body behind. That's when I feel most at peace. One minute I'm sitting securely in one world—at a bar, say, or a dinner party—and the next, without warning, I'm out of place, out of time, somehow removed from everyone around me. When I was small, my mother called me her ethereal child. "You don't really live in this world," she'd say, kissing the top of my head.

The back of my throat swelled. The tequila was making me uneven, off-kilter. No wonder I rarely drank liquor. In front of me, water from melted ice puddled the bar. I ran a finger through it, stretched a thin stream outward. Around me, people were gathering their coats, their hats, getting ready to leave. The bartender, her back to me, was wiping down the back counter with a cloth. Suddenly the bar seemed dank, depressing.

I looked down. The matchbook had fallen to the floor. I bent down, scooped it up, folded the thin cardboard between my fingers. There were two utterly distinct worlds, weren't there? There was the physical—the cardboard in my palm, the wetness of the bar, the tequila that still scorched my throat. Yes, this was the world I could touch, feel—but there was more behind it.

In my mind I saw again the burly man as he tossed his matchbook in my lap. Perhaps, drunk as he was, he had felt the split of worlds. Perhaps, stumbling home, he had watched the red of the traffic lights dance, closed his arms against the cold, wondered what else was out there. Perhaps he had fumbled with the keys to his door, fallen in a heap on the couch, closed his eyes in relief. Now he could disappear.

Shall I take his offering as a sign? Shall I count the letters he scrawled, map them to a hidden world? I took a breath, and then another. I said the four letters of God's name very quietly, almost in a whisper. I imagined doing it for thirty-five hours. *Yud. Heh. Vav. Heh.*

I could feel my own heart beating.

Why mysticism? What did I want? What did anyone want from religion? Dynamism. Mystery. Hope. Contact. Knowledge.

"Religion is a metaphor for God," my friend Mark McCormick once said. "It's part of an endless poem that's both personal and universal, that has no beginning and no end, that's deeply connected with language, with thought, but is equally resonant with the body."

It struck me that Mark—who wasn't even an official Jew yet—was the closest thing I had to a religious community. Mark, who spoke with me about the twists and turns of Judaism, about what kind of Jew he would become, about the meaning of religion itself. Once we'd even prayed together. It was a prayer for strength in the face of shame, I think. We'd asked for the strength to find who we are, and love who we are; and afterwards, sitting next to him, I felt different.

Now, in the bar, harsh ceiling lights flashed on and then off and then on again. The bartender, a heavyset woman already tired in her twenties, turned and looked at me. She blew a piece of hair from her face. "Girlfriend," she said, leaning over to wipe up my area, "I think it's time for you to head home."

Home. And I thought of David, and of how I would crawl under the covers, nudge him awake, tell him the story of my evening.

And then I was stepping forward, and then I was outside; footfall after footfall, feeling the ground beneath my feet, licking my lips against the wind, reaching out to touch what I could, the cold windows of parked cars, the rough blackness of a metal rail, I wasn't drunk but felt as though I was—or perhaps I was—I could have spun round, could have seen the sidewalk tremble. I was no longer myself, I was the man with a message at the bar, I was Mark McCormick choosing his Hebrew name, I was one of the ancient kabbalists molding a golem out of wet clay in the middle of the night, and suddenly I knew them all intimately, knew they were all part of the same endless poem, as surely as I knew myself.

KOSHER—ME?

Ryn Wood had the tip of a pen in her mouth. She sat on the half-finished floor at Pasta Bella, scowling, her back against the wall, her bent knees supporting a large notebook. Chest-high boxes filled the dining area. Wood dust coated the floor, speckled the walls. Her restaurant would open in two weeks and she needed, at the very least, to finalize the menu items. Now. I'd been summoned to her there in Sonoma, between a large pizza oven and a concrete countertop, to give moral support and to produce names, pronto. She tossed me a Coke, gratis, to spur rapid-fire delivery.

"No pressure," she said, "but I need to finish this in five minutes."

"Right." I sipped, stared at the list of dishes in front of me, figured I'd start with the obvious. "What about calling the lasagna, say, Lasagna? And then you could call the fettuccine Fettuccine. And so on. You can't miss."

She blanched. "I hope you're being funny. If not, you're going to have to pay for that Coke." She focused again on the notebook. I waited. Through the window I saw a delivery truck careen into the parking lot, swerve around the rock garden, screech to a halt.

"Expecting something important?" I asked.

"Tables would be nice, a radical approach to dining," she said without lifting her head. She took a deep breath. Then her pen began to move furiously.

"Got it," she yelled, looking up. "I'm naming all the menu items after my friends."

"Won't work," I said. "You have only two Italian friends."

"So what? Everything—the appetizers, entrées, desserts—they'll all be named after my friends." She ticked off names on her fingers. "There's Mako and Luna. There's Susie Murray. And Mark—I'll turn him into the baby clams. There's The Vivi—that'll be olive tapenade and goat cheese on homemade focaccia." She looked at me. "Then there's Lisa Schiffman."

"You're kidding, right? You can't name a dish Lisa Schiffman."

"Why not?"

"You just can't. Call it something like Linguine Lisa, maybe. But don't use my last name—nobody will order the dish. It's an *Italian* restaurant, for God's sake. My surname won't fit."

"Why?"

"For obvious reasons."

"The Big J again?"

I nodded.

"Get over it."

"I can't. What if you have a bunch of anti-Semites for customers? Leave my name out of it. If you want a Jewish name for an Italian dish, call it the Oy Vaygelah. It sounds vaguely Italian."

"Don't be crazy," she said calmly, going back to her pad. "I want you on the menu. Listen to this. 'Lisa Schiffman: delicious grilled free-range chicken with prosciutto in sage cream sauce over linguine.'"

"Prosciutto? You're putting my name on a dish made with *pig*? A dish that mixes milk and meat?" I'm strangely, unpredictably appalled. "It's not kosher."

Ryn stared at me, surprised, then laughed. "And last time I checked," she said, getting up to meet the deliverymen, "neither were you."

That was the final straw, I think. The word *kosher*, which had always kept a comfortable distance from me, a cousin once-removed, began to infiltrate my consciousness in a big way.

It was suddenly everywhere. The supermarket became a vast architectural container for the word. At the Safeway I nabbed a cart, pretended to be shopping. Instead, I hunted down foods marked kosher. I looked for labels touting either an encirled U, the stamp of approval from the Union of Orthodox Jewish Congregations, or an encirled k. It didn't take me long.

In the breakfast aisle: Cheerios, Cocoa Puffs, Total, Wheaties, Corn Flakes, Froot Loops, Rice Krispies, Maypo, Shredded Wheat, Cap'n Crunch—all kosher. In the candy aisle: Baby Ruth, all Cadbury's flavors, Hershey's Kisses, M&M's, Almond Joy, Mounds, Reese's Peanut Butter Cups, and my personal chocolate of choice, Toblerone. In the cookie aisle I was pleased to see that my habitual cookies got the Orthodox thumbs-up: Nutter Butters, Grasshoppers, Pepperidge Farm Double Chocolate Milanos. Even Oreos were kosher.

That wasn't all. In the soda aisle, more. Coke, 7-Up, Dr Pepper, Hawaiian Punch, Snapple, Arizona Teas, A&W root beer, Orange Crush, Canada Dry ginger ale, Fanta. I paused for a millisecond in front of Tab—was it? Did it have to be? Yes. So was Folgers coffee, Grey Poupon mustard, Heinz ketchup, Baco Bits, Contadina marinara sauce, all the Ortega salsas. I sped through the aisles, my head swiveling right and left. Suddenly I stopped. What about Chinese food? I turned the cart, headed east, landed in front of Canton chow mein noodles and egg roll skins. Kosher. So were China Pack's duck sauces and hot mustards, La Choy Chinese vegetables, Seasons Oriental vegetables, and Mrs. Adler's hoison and soy sauces.

What, exactly, did it mean to eat kosher? I developed a few questions over the next few days, then aimed and fired them at Jews I knew. Do you feel uncomfortable eating ham? A little? What about a cheeseburger? When was the last time you ate pork? Do you keep kosher in the house? Yes? Then what about outside? Didn't you devour a container of pork fried rice last week at Chow Lum Palace? Do you always keep kosher? Yes? What about that Barbados vacation, when the crabmeat-stuffed lobster-claw dinner highlighted the buffet table? Oh. Right. Perhaps you're kind of kosher. Ever heard of eco-kosher? Glatt kosher?

These questions were just the tip of the iceberg. There were more. Many more. Where did it all begin—at Sinai? Back then, was keeping kosher a way to protect yourself from harm, from health risks? Or, as you trudged through the desert bearing a pack on your shoulders and a child in your arms, was keeping kosher yet another reminder that you and your people were separate, different from God's other children? What, exactly, were the food prohibitions, and why the hyperconsciousness about what and how you ate? Hygiene? Holiness? Separateness?

You want answers? You need time. You could do the work: sit down, sweat it out with the books of Leviticus and Deuteronomy, then with Maimonides, the medieval medical doctor and rabbi. You could get a translation of the *Zohar*, see for yourself what the mystics said about the Jewish way of eating. You could immerse yourself in anthropological theory, read Mary Douglas on the meaning of ritual pollution. You could, horror of horrors, try keeping kosher.

Supermarket products aside, I wanted origins. I wanted the text. I schlepped to the Jewish Community Library in San Francisco, lugged home three different translations of Leviticus. I scooped out a bowl of Ben & Jerry's Chunky Monkey®, headed for the center of the living room rug, and read the regs until my eyesight blurred. Here, because I'm detail-oriented, is nearly the whole megillah. My favorite compulsions are in bold.

LEVITICUS XI

² These are the living things which you may eat among all the beasts that are on the earth. ³ Whatever parts the hoof and is cloven-footed and chews the cud, among these animals, you may eat. ⁴ Nevertheless among those that chew the cud or part the hoof, you shall not eat these: **The camel, because it chews the cud but does not part the hoof, is unclean to you.**

⁵ And the rock badger, because it chews the cud but does not part the hoof, is unclean to you. ⁶ And the hare, because it chews the cud but does not part the hoof, is unclean to you. ⁷ **And the swine, because it parts the hoof and is cloven-footed but does not chew the cud, is unclean to you.** ⁸ Of their flesh you shall not eat, and their carcasses you shall not touch; they are unclean to you.

⁹ These you may eat, of all that are in the waters. **Everything in the waters that has fins and scales, whether in the seas or the rivers, you may eat.** ¹⁰ **But anything in the seas or the rivers that has not fins and scales, of the swarming creatures in the waters and of the living creatures that are in the waters, is an abomination to you.** ¹¹ They shall remain an abomination to you; of their flesh you shall not eat, and their carcasses you shall have in abomination. ¹² Everything in the waters that has not fins and scales is an abomination to you.

¹³ **And these you shall have in abomination among the birds, they shall not be eaten, they are an abomination: the eagle, the vulture, the osprey,** ¹⁴ **the kite, the falcon according to its kind,** ¹⁵ **every raven according to its kind,** ¹⁶ **the ostrich, the nighthawk, the sea gull, the hawk according to its kind,** ¹⁷ **the owl, the cormorant, the ibis,** ¹⁸ **the water hen, the pelican, the carrion vulture,** ¹⁹ **the stork, the heron according to its kind, the hoopoe, and the bat.**

²⁰ **All winged insects that go on all fours are an abomination to you.** ²¹ Yet among the winged insects that go on all fours you may eat those which have legs above their feet, with which to leap on the earth. ²² **Of them you may eat: the locust according to its kind, the bald locust according to its kind, the cricket according to its kind, and the grasshopper according to its kind.** ²³ **But all other winged insects which have four feet are an abomination to you.**

²⁴ And by these you shall become unclean; whoever touches their carcass shall be unclean until the evening, ²⁵ and whoever carries any part of their carcass shall wash his clothes and be unclean until the evening. ²⁶ Every animal which parts the hoof but is not cloven-footed or does not chew the cud is unclean to you; everyone who touches them shall be unclean. ²⁷ **And all that go on their paws, among the animals that go on all fours, are unclean to you; whoever touches their carcass shall be unclean until the evening,** ²⁸ and he who carries their carcass shall wash his clothes and be unclean until the evening; they are unclean to you.

²⁹ **And these are unclean to you among the swarming things that swarm upon the earth: the weasel, the mouse, the great lizard according**

to its kind, ³⁰ the gecko, the land crocodile, the lizard, the sand lizard, and the chameleon. ³¹ These are unclean to you among all that swarm; whoever touches them when they are dead shall be unclean until the evening. . . .

⁴¹ Every swarming thing that swarms upon the earth is an abomination; it shall not be eaten. ⁴² **Whatever goes on its belly, and whatever goes on all fours, or whatever has many feet, all the swarming things that swarm upon the earth, you shall not eat; for they are an abomination.**

Shall I simplify? You can't eat eels. They slither through the sea without fins or scales. You can eat some locusts, but not others. You can eat a grasshopper and a cricket. You can eat a goat but not a weasel. Don't eat snakes or worms, things that belly over the land. No crocodile, even if the breast is batter-fried. And no camel meat.

Swordfish is controversial. The big *machers*—the big shots—are involved in an argument. Some say the fish is kosher; others, not. Swordfish apparently has scales—bony tubercles, to be exact—when young, then loses them later on in life. Volumes have been written about the issue.

Broccoli, too, sparks a brouhaha. Bugs can hide too easily, burrow down into the soft green heads. And bugs—most of them, anyway—aren't kosher. A year or two ago an inordinate number of Jews were finding these little critters in their boiled broccoli. The Powers That Be sent out a Kosher Alert. Oy! One of the head rabbis in Israel finally put his foot down, told his people to steer clear of the evil little trees.

Yes, there are temptations, prohibited delights: the soft white flesh of broiled scallops, the cold baby shrimp you sink in cocktail sauce then suck from their casing, the king crab legs dipped in butter, the honey-roasted ham so smooth it takes away your breath, the hot crunch of morning bacon between your teeth. Beef burgers, moist and pink inside, drenched with melted cheddar.

If you took any of these succulent morsels into your mouth, would you have a moment of guilt, a split-second flash of Jew-consciousness inside your head? As you bit down, would a tiny voice shout *it's not kosher?*

Ashley, a woman in the category of not-quite-a-friend, invited me to a dinner party recently. I said yes. I arrived, schmoozed, sat down to dinner. The main dish was roasted pork loin. The skin was brown and crusty with a bit of fat underneath. I looked at the meat on my plate, prodded it lightly with my fork. I paused. I told myself not to be ridiculous. *You're not kosher,* I thought, *so eat.*

I speared the meat, bit down. That's when my Inner Jew rose up with a vengeance. Every time I chewed, I saw the image of an enormous, grunting, filthy pig inside my head.

Bite. The pig snorted, pawed the ground. Chew. The pig slopped dinner scraps from a garbage trough. Ugh.

I put my fork down softly, hoping no one would notice.

No such luck.

"Is something wrong?" Ashley asked politely.

"No, nothing." I was chipper, ever so bright. "It's delicious!"

"But you've stopped eating. You don't like the pork?"

All heads turned. The clatter of forks ceased.

"No. It's not that. The meat's perfect. Really."

She stared at me. "What's up?"

I stiffened. "It's just that . . . I . . . um . . . I don't usually eat pork."

"You don't — oh." Immediate discomfort. Her face reddened. "Are you . . ." Deep breath. "Are you *kosher?* I didn't know. I'm sorry." The man next to me shifted, reached for his water glass.

"Kosher? Me? Not at all. I, um, don't eat much meat of any kind. Here," I said overloudly, reaching for a plate of scalloped potatoes, "I'll fill up on the vegetables. Joe, more starch?" I turned to the man next to me, offered up the dish. The conversation around me resumed. Ashley smiled in a strained sort of way.

How could I have explained? What could I have said, in truth? *No, I'm not kosher. Well, yes, maybe I am. Kind of. It's an assimilated-Jewish thing. Pork freaks me out. Shrimp is fine. Lobster's fine. Right.*

I know. I can't explain why pork sets off the alarm. But I know I'm not alone. Ask another Jew. Ask her, over there in the corner seat. I bet she's Jewish. Ask her if she's experiencing any sort of side effects—unease, discomfort, pangs of guilt—between bites.

What's up with that? We're a nation of closeted Jews. We appear to be eating blithely at McDonald's, at Arby's, at Joanne's House of Ribs, but inside, we're making deals with ourselves. *I can eat a Quarter Pounder, but not a Quarter Pounder with cheese.* Inside, we're keeping alive the secret lines of demarcation.

We're exhibiting what my friend Lauren calls kosher behavior. She's a psychologist with a master's in theology, so I trust her to target this sort of psycho-theological disorder correctly.

"I do it myself," she said. We were in her kitchen. She waved a half-peeled banana in my direction. "I pride myself on never having taken a bite of pork in my life. But am I kosher? Religious even? No. Not at all. But I'm a Jew. And certain foods remind me I'm a Jew. It's a weird psychological residue, something maybe left over from biblical times."

She put down the banana absentmindedly. "I'm not saying it makes sense. But that's the way it is." She opened the fridge. She bent over, stuck her head in, began searching for something. I could tell that her mind was still revved. "You know," a muffled voice said from the chilly depths, "you could do an experiment. You could keep kosher for awhile."

I was silent.

She pulled her head out. A small green leaf, a piece of spinach or lettuce perhaps, clung to her hair. Her hand now held an avocado. "No. Now I've got it. You could go in the other direction. Keep totally *not* kosher." Suddenly, she was shouting. "Eat pork every day for a week. That's it. You should eat pig every day and see how you feel." Triumph. Her face was flushed.

She continued. "I'm telling you to construct a test for yourself. *Approach that which you fear, that which makes you uncomfortable.* It's done all the time in psychology. We call it paradoxical reconditioning. If you were afraid of dirt, we'd have you stick your hand into a garbage pail ten times a day."

I laughed. "So. You believe in the power of paradox."

She looked surprised. "It works. If you have an aversion to something, repetitive exposure will wipe out the aversion. It allows you to look at the problem closely. Take this whole pork thing. Is it a knee-jerk reaction, some superficial sign of your Judaism? Or is it something deeper, some reflection of a deep Jewish spirituality?"

"How should I know?" I said. "Why do I have to be the test pig?"

"Hey," she said, putting down the avocado. She grabbed a pile of take-out menus, tossed me a few off the top. "I'm starving. We need food. What'll it be?"

I shrugged, didn't miss a beat. "Josie's Back Bay?"

Lauren smiled. "Aha! Barbecued pork ribs. It appears the test is about to begin."

I didn't end up eating pork that night. I picked at fried chicken wings, collard greens, and coleslaw, washed it all down with a Cherry Coke®. Over the next few days I mulled over the idea of the test. Should I do it? Was it ridiculous? Could I learn something?

Back home I thought of the American anthropologist Clifford Geertz. In *The Interpretation of Cultures*, Geertz, aligning himself with Max Weber, said that man is an animal suspended in webs of significance he himself has spun.

I was certainly stuck in a web. Why had I imbued pork, but not lobster, with Jewish meaning? Did eating pork really have anything to do with being Jewish? As I jotted notes at the back of the Geertz book, two questions occurred to me: In whose web was I caught? And wasn't it time to weave a web of my own?

I decided to conduct the test.

Day 1. Pork fried rice. I thought I'd start small, give myself a break. Chopsticks in hand, head bent over the paper container, I shoveled.

Tiny squares of meat spotted the rice. Hardly a challenge. I ate alone, standing in my kitchen. The dog stared at me mournfully. I was glad that David wasn't around. I didn't want him to see this pathetic ritual.

Day 2. Bacon strips. No problem. David and I were at the Rockridge Café for breakfast. His head was buried in the *New York Times*. I ordered a tofu scramble and then a side of bacon. David lowered the paper. "Bacon?"

"Sure, why not?" I said. I tried to sound casual.

"Bacon?" he repeated. He looked from me to the waitress and then back again.

The waitress, a sweet young thing with nails painted black, eyed us with amusement. I nodded. "That's what I said. A side of bacon." I turned to David. "Any reason I shouldn't order that?"

He looked at me intently. He fingered the edge of the table. Finally, he shrugged. "No, not really. I guess it just seemed like a very . . . *unusual* thing for you to do." Then, without another word, he buried his head back in the news.

The waitress scribbled something down and left.

The bacon arrived. Crunch. It was sweet. Innocent, somehow. Not really pork.

Day 3. Pastrami and melted Swiss. I pulled back the top slice of bread, examined the meat beneath. Thin strands of fat traversed the surface. I lowered the bread again, covering meat, cheese, and mustard. Mark McCormick, tunafish sandwich in hand, stared at me. He had two weeks to go before his conversion, before the mikvah that would officially make him a Jew.

"It gives me a weird feeling," he said.

"What?"

"The thought of eating pastrami and cheese. I couldn't do it. Separate, they're fine. I could eat pastrami alone, ham alone, bacon alone. But with dairy? It's the whole milk-and-meat thing. You aren't supposed to eat a kid boiled in its mother's milk. It makes sense to me. I connect to it at a very primal level."

"So you're saying you wouldn't eat a cheeseburger?"

"You mean a beef burger with cheese?"

"I guess."

"No. Definitely not." Pause. "But, I *would* eat a turkey burger with cheese."

"Enlighten me."

He leaned toward me over the table. "A turkey burger with cheese wouldn't be eating a kid cooked in its mother's milk. You see?"

I bit down. Mark stared at me. I chewed. Mark unscrewed the top of his Snapple ®. I felt a vague, faraway pang of something. Was it guilt? Nausea? The biblical residue of ancestral law? I kept on chewing.

Day 4. Pork loin. This was the big time. The real thing. A thick, juicy slab of roasted pig. I was sitting alone at a restaurant counter downtown. The plate of flesh arrived, with potatoes swimming in meat juice. Had I really ordered this? The scent of wet dog rose like steam from the plate.

I carved out a delicate piece. **Jew.**

I forked it into my mouth. **Jew.**

I looked around. No one else at the counter looked up from their midday specials. I felt strange. Maybe I had some sort of weird Oliver Sacks–type disease, something neurologically based, a psycho-religious reversal: eating pork made me feel Jewish.

My stomach tightened. I kept going, forking in piece after piece, chewing, nearly drowning in the taste and smell of that pig. Even my iced tea tasted like pork loin. The odor dominated the air, forcing me to turn my head away when I took a breath.

I left, leaving a large tip, an offering to the gods.

• • •

Day 5. Edmund Leach, an English anthropologist, once said that we engage in rituals to transmit collective messages to ourselves. I believe this. And I also believe Mary Douglas, who said rituals of purity and impurity impose order upon a chaotic world. As humans, she said, we are constantly performing gestures of classification and separation, constantly reordering our world to make it conform to an idea.

Today was my day for pork chops. My stomach yowled in protest. I looked down at my belly, told myself pork chops were no more impure than chicken breasts. I grabbed a chop in one hand, bit down, tugged the meat away from the bone. It was sweet, tender. I'd never felt more Jewish. I savored the taste, the transgression. I took the leftovers home.

Day 6. Leftover pork chops. I was on the phone with my sister, whose call had interrupted my meal.

"You're doing what? The *opposite* of kosher?"

I swallowed, moved the receiver closer to my mouth. "Yeah. Like right now I'm eating pork chops."

"Gross." Pause. "Why don't you try to *keep* kosher? Wait—let me guess. It's the four sets of dishes."

I grabbed a chop by the bone, dipped it in applesauce. "Four?"

"One for milk, one for meat, two for Passover."

I pulled at the pork with my teeth, tore off a chunk, kept talking. She was my sister; I could talk with my mouth full.

I said, "Since when do you know about kosher?"

"What? Gross. Could you next time chew first, please? My ex-roommate is kosher. Remember Susie? After she and Eric married and moved in together, she divided up the whole kitchen. It's unbelievable. She and Eric are like zealots. Two refrigerators. Two stoves. Milk dishes, meat dishes, Passover dishes. All the silverware—again, in two. And she carts it all to the mikvah to be dunked clean."

"Insane," I said.

"No, that's not insane. This is insane—" She paused for dramatic effect. "They're not kosher when they leave the house."

I stopped my last chop in midair, just before my mouth. I laughed, and it went on and on until suddenly something within me sank. I quieted. In the window I saw my partial reflection. A thin hand waved a pork chop against the backdrop of night.

"Hey," my sister said. "You still there?"

I was silent. Thinking. Who was I to judge someone else's religious contradictions? I lowered the chop down to the plate.

"Yup," I said, "I'm here. I'm still wherever I was." My head felt heavy. "I think my mood's about to spiral."

"Look," she said, "it's the chemicals. Christ. Just think about the steroids in that piece of pork. The hormones, the antibiotics. Your body can't process it all. You've been eating meat every day. Take a break already."

She was right. I needed to kick back. Day 7 could wait.

What then? The obvious. The next day I began to learn about ritual slaughter. First I saw a film about it. Then I started frequenting my local kosher butcher. Afterwards, I read. Reading about the kosher rules of slaughter became a strange compulsion, an embarrassing tic, a habit worse than obsessive hand-washing. Once, on the bathroom floor, David found a slightly waterlogged booklet called *Make It Kosher Meat.*

Another time, shoved into the deli drawer of the fridge, he found the torn page of a book—a drawing of a cow. The cow, a bewildered-looking thing, was divided into numbered sections. Some sections, like numbers one, two, and three, were kosher. Other sections weren't. I watched David stare at the drawing intently. Then he reached for a plate and carefully arranged the drawing on it, as though it were a chunk of Brie. Waiter-style, he balanced the plate on his fingertips, walked it out to where I was sitting, bent over me.

"Your cow, madam."

For the record: loin is a no-no. So is rump, shank, flank, filet mignon, sirloin, tenderloin, T-bone, and porterhouse steak. In other words, religious Jews don't eat butt. The meat near the sciatic nerve is off-limits (unless the nerve has been removed, a process so expensive that it almost never happens in the United States). The prohibition has something to do with Jacob's sciatic nerve being touched by an . . . um, angel. Don't ask. It's in Genesis 32:32.

Then there's the slaughter itself, done by someone trained, devout, careful. This someone, usually a man, is called a *shochet*. He's considered a religious official of sorts, perhaps a rabbi of death. This man understands the law. He knows this: there will be no smashing of heads. Why? You can't shoot or scald an animal to death. Stabbing is likewise forbidden. You can't artificially stun the animal before slaughter with a blow to the head, an electric shock, or a tranquilizer injection. Jewish law about kosher slaughter reflects a sense of ethics, a deep regard for the ending of life, a determination to avoid causing pain to another sentient being.

How to kill according to God's will? You have to summon a sense of the holy. Before you plunge the blade, you say a blessing. You actually pray to God. Then you slice the animal's throat, kill it instantly by severing the jugular vein, trachea, and esophagus in a single, uninterrupted stroke. You can't pause. Even a momentary delay, a slight hesitation, invalidates the kill. No. You have to cut off the blood supply to the animal's brain at once, minimize the potential for pain. As the shochet, your knife must be without flaw. Not a single nick can mar the blade, risk tearing the neck of the animal. The cut has to be perfect every time. And so it is.

Day 7. Chicken with prosciutto in sage cream sauce.

Pasta Bella. The place was mobbed. I dodged elbows and small children, wove my way between tables, made it to the kitchen where chef Ryn Wood bent over a sizzling pan.

"Hey, you," I yelled over the din.

She turned, wooden spoon in hand, saw me, smiled, and shouted, "LISA SCHIFFMAN."

Therese, a waitress standing nearby, looked up, sprang into action. She grabbed a plate. "Who gets it?" she yelled to Ryn.

"Gets what?" Ryn was puzzled.

Therese shifted her foot, poised for flight. "Lisa Schiffman."

Nobody moved. Ryn caught my eye. I suppressed a smile.

"Sweetheart," she said to Therese, "we've got this dish in the flesh. She *is* Lisa Schiffman. The real person. Tell her how many people order her entrée."

Therese brightened, looked at me. "You! I hear your name fifty times a day. The lunch ladies. The poker guys. The office crowd."

I smiled.

"Personally, you're a bit too rich for my taste. I can ever eat only half."

Ryn glared.

I hugged her, then tweaked her cap. "So where's my commission? My royalties? The Jerry Garcia estate gets a percentage of every quart of Cherry Garcia sold."

She tilted her head back and laughed. "That's it. I quit. Even my friends want money from me now." She began to untie her apron. "I need a break. Marcos? Ready? Your turn on the line."

A young man, one of her cooks, looked up from the sidelines where he was slicing tomatoes. "I just had to dump nearly a whole case of these," he said.

Ryn stiffened. She motioned him over to her. Together they leaned over the pan, where she explained something to him carefully, then slipped the spoon into his hand. He listened intently, nodding his head.

Ryn turned to me. "Outside? The garden? I'll meet you there in a sec."

I headed out back, to the garden — or, in real estate parlance, the Exclusive Private Outdoor Area! — shared by Ryn and her employees.

It was a patch of cement large enough for a bench, a dumpster, and a potted plant. And it was enclosed by an eight-foot-high wooden fence. I sat on the bench, which offered an unparalleled frontal view of the dumpster. Ryn blasted out the back door shortly, a packet of tobacco and matches in one hand and rolling paper in the other.

"I want a cigarette," I said, on impulse. I had smoked once, when I was twelve.

She looked at me in surprise. "Sure. And then you'll collapse. How about we share mine?"

I nodded and watched her sprinkle tobacco carefully into the fold of the paper. "Did you see what happened back there, in the kitchen? With Marcos? I had to bite my tongue, then explain it all to him carefully."

"Explain what?"

"The way we talk about food. Maybe it's because of the way I was trained, at Tassajara, by the monks. Buddhists believe—and I do too—that handling food is a religious experience. At a monastery, being head of the kitchen is one of the highest honors. So you'd never say, 'I dumped the tomatoes.' You dump trash, not food."

Ryn paused to lick the edge of the rolling paper, sealing the cigarette. "Yesterday Therese asked me what she should do with all this *stuff*. And I looked at her—she was holding a case of beautiful fresh herbs. Rosemary. Thyme. Cilantro. I smelled these incredible scents. And I thought to myself, *stuff?*" She leaned back on the bench. "*Stuff?* I took a breath, tried to explain to her that we don't refer to rosemary that way."

"And?"

"And guess what? She looked at me like I was a nut." She laughed, then took a drag. "Maybe I am. Here," she said, passing me the cigarette. "Be a hero."

I took the butt. I flashed on the time Ryn had guided me through an upscale kitchen store. Back then, both jobless—"in between jobs" was what we said—we were driving around the East Bay. It was late afternoon and we were killing time. I'd asked her to tell me why some pots are better than others.

Stop. Screech. Ryn had turned the truck around, headed for Sur La Table, where on a two-hour journey she'd toured me through the subtleties of copper, iron, and Calphalon, then blanching and boiling, cheesecloth and cutting boards, the necessity of having both a wooden and a rubber spatula. She'd prepared nearly an entire meal in there, an imaginary vegetarian feast, and I'd been her eager student.

I brought the butt to my lips, inhaled, doubled over in a spasm of coughing. Ryn stared out at the vast expanse of dumpster, waited calmly for the return of her cigarette.

"I trained at Tassajara for two years," she said. "Every day I sat zazen as part of my training to become a chef. Every day was a form of practice for me. Slowly, the way I touched food changed. Slowly, the way I thought about food, spoke about food, envisioned food — it all changed. A shift happened."

She took the butt, inhaled, then exhaled in a slow stream. "Don't tell anyone I said this — it's way too corny — but food became holy. Sacred. So," she said, looking at the back door, "even though this place can drive me up the wall, it's a reminder."

"A reminder of what?"

"God, maybe. Presence, maybe. Depends on the moment. Hey —" She dropped the butt, ground the last of it under her heel, tossed the shreds into the dumpster. "Break's over," she said. "I need to get back to work, and you need to eat."

Ryn ushered me through the back door and onto a chair at the edge of the counter. Therese strode over, notebook in hand. I ordered — what else? Myself.

It was Day 7, for all intents and purposes. At the counter, I waited for my food to arrive. Around me, people were eating, tearing off pieces of warm focaccia, twirling fettuccine on the tines of forks, scooping the soft meat out of clamshells. Shortly, I would be eating prosciutto, a permutation of pig. Shortly, I would mix milk and meat, savor a cream sauce. Suddenly, the thought made me ill. My stomach churned, turned over once.

After today, would I go back to what Lauren referred to as kosher behavior? Would I avoid pork? I tipped back my water glass, sipped, let the ice strike my teeth. The history of Judaism from its origins until now could be written either as a history of law or as mystery, asserted Leo Baeck, a rabbi and philosopher who survived the camps. If you followed law—commandment, according to Baeck— you'd look to the Torah for authority, and you'd believe that the dietary prohibitions were commandments of God. If you reveled in mystery, you'd look to the *Zohar*, the text of the Jewish mystical tradition. You'd believe, perhaps, that eating kosher food was a mystical path, a way to nurture the essence of God, a way to begin the healing of the universe.

My teeth crunched down on a piece of ice. Somewhere, a shochet's blade was slicing the neck of a cow. Somewhere, a Jew was sitting in McDonald's, devouring a cheeseburger. Here, in a small town in northern California, I was making it through my seventh day of conscious nonkosherness.

That morning I'd read something revolutionary. Judaism, said Baeck, was a religion of paradox and reconciliation. The thought freed me. Why had I expected Judaism to be rational, logical? Why had I believed that the way I expressed my Judaism—the way any Jew expressed it—should be without contradiction? Paradox was an inherent part of being a Jew. It was a constant. Yet that didn't preclude the idea of reconciliation.

Therese arrived, set the plate down in front of me.

Approach that which makes you uncomfortable, Lauren had said. Reconcile.

Would I ever keep kosher? Why should I? Would it be about hygiene? No. The FDA already protected me. Would it be about separateness? No. I wanted my life to be inclusive of others, not exclusive. I wanted to be able to break bread with my husband, my mother, my father. None of them was kosher.

I looked down at the piece of chicken. Ryn had delicately cradled the meat in cream sauce. Every time she prepared something, she had the presence of mind to attend to the details. Holiness. Yes. If I became kosher, it would be about finding holiness in the small, mundane places I usually missed. It would be about being aware.

I often wonder if I've lost some sort of vital connection to my life. I eat as I read. I eat as I write. I eat in the car sometimes, peeling back a layer of foil and biting down on whatever's there. I eat with partial attention, or none at all.

I pressed my knife against the meat, then sliced evenly through the breast.

Here was the paradox: Judaism, the religion of the book, understood that life must be lived. It knew that text could only go so far. It knew the sound a blade made as it cut an animal's throat. It understood how holiness could live at my table.

Just then I heard Judaism call to me. *Break bread with me,* it said. *Be with me. Taste.*

THE GLeanInGs

t ell me about the gleanings," I said. I was at Café Macondo, facing Rabbi Litman, her cup of tea, and her triangle of chocolate layer cake. The café, a dim joint with mismatched chairs and cheap wooden tables, was a favorite hangout of mine. I liked to watch people linger there. Some talked to friends for hours, waving their arms for emphasis; some labored, red pen in hand, groaning over mysterious sheaves of typewritten pages; and others sat quietly alone, staring out into the distance. Eventually, just to prevent the café from going broke, a few would relent, reach into their tired pockets, pay for coffee or a muffin.

"Again with the gleanings?" she said.

"Yes. This time I'll write it all down." I bent purposefully over my pad, wobbling the rickety table and knocking my pen to the floor. The rabbi looked at me kindly. As I bent to retrieve the pen, a question assaulted me: *Why are you, once again, looking for answers outside yourself?* I was thirty-four. I should know more. I should be larger in my own life.

"Your pen is ready?" Rabbi Litman warmed her hands around the cup of tea. She was an experienced rabbi and a professor of history. This meant she was a learned, credentialed storyteller. Her passion for the stories of her people was so deep, so persistent, it formed a kind of architecture. It seemed to give her inner life an invincible structure.

"Yes. Ready."

Rabbi Litman settled in her seat, sipped at her mint tea, and began. "The time is soon before the destruction of the second temple, or perhaps just afterwards. The Jews are under Roman occupation. The Romans exercise their power vigorously and effectively. It becomes clear to a small group of rabbis that they're about to lose a huge body of religious wisdom — wisdom that traditionally had been passed on orally. Now the rabbis realize they must do what they've never done: they must write it down."

"They'd never written down the wisdom of their people?"

"No. Judaism had been an oral tradition. This meant that it had great creative potential. It was unfixed, moving, interactive. But the rabbis feared that they would lose essential wisdom. They understood that the spoken word was ephemeral and believed that their religion needed a written foundation."

"But why?"

"Imagine the time in which they lived. They had an untenable relationship with the Romans. They were repeatedly under siege. As the power of Christianity increased, so did the systematic suppression of Jewish life. Roman conduct went beyond petty persecution. The lives of the Jews were being undermined."

The rabbi paused. She had an excellent sense of timing. She took another sip of tea before she spoke. "They wanted to secure their religion. This makes perfect sense to me. These rabbis, they went out into the world and engaged in a process they called 'the gleanings.' They went into the countryside and questioned common people, scholars, everyone and anyone who was a Jew. They gleaned from everyone their wisdom about Judaism, about Jewish practices. *What did your mother say? What did your father say? What did your father's mother say?* And they wrote down the answers. In this way, they compiled books of rules for how to live as a Jew. This became the mishnah, the oral torah."

She smiled. I stopped my pen, gathered my thoughts. There was a process known as the gleanings. This much I understood. There was something called an oral torah—only it was written down. Right. Made perfect sense. This kind of logic showed exactly why trying to figure out Judaism could drive someone crazy.

Rabbi Litman said the oral torah was an important part of the Talmud—and that, I knew, was one of the central pillars of Jewish life. It was a book that dared address the nature of all things in an effort to seek out truth. But truth troubled me. I never knew which truth to believe.

The rabbi started up again. "The ancient rabbis said the wisdom they gathered came straight from Moses. They said it was given to Moses alongside the written Torah. Then it was passed down in multiple forms." She shrugged. "I can't tell if they really believed this was true or if it was a symbolic statement."

She delicately pressed her fork through the piece of cake. Over time, what I had come to admire about her was this: her grace in the face of life's insistent turbulence. Each day the rabbi—who stood the slippery ground between Reform and Reconstructionist Judaism, who had once, in her interpretation of a holy book, so angered another rabbi that he'd wanted to strike her, who answered to a congregation as moody and forceful as the sea—understood that her faith would clarify itself, would continue to cloud and then clear. She knew that from this clouding and clearing emerged a kind of wisdom.

"Have you ever read the Talmud?" she asked.

I shook my head no.

"It's quite amazing. There are dialogues, trialogues, quadralogues. People across the generations discuss all sorts of things. People who were never in a room together engage a subject. It's very free-form. It holds dreams and tells stories. It shares recipes, explains charms for healing, comments on astronomy. It's wild, really—a highly symbolic, imaginative, and associative literature. A great mistake many people make in reading it is to literalize it. And it's just not meant to be literalized."

I lifted my pen, made a note. *Find the Talmud in a translation I can understand.* I was tempted to encourage the rabbi to keep moving along this path of discussion but felt that something was still unfinished. Something from before.

"Back to the gleanings?" I asked.

"Why not?" she said.

"What have you gleaned?"

This woman whose life was devoted to Judaism put down her fork. Cocking her head, she smiled. "Lisa, it's time to turn the tables. So tell me," she said, leaning forward, "what have *you* gleaned?"

Can we revise our personal histories? Reshape the stories — sculpting here, touching up there — that describe our lives? Sometimes I want to. I want, for example, to say that the afternoon tea with the rabbi ended on a high note. I want to say that I put down my pen, told her what I'd gleaned, tied together my stray strands of Judaism in an articulate way.

Perhaps that was the moment at which I declared myself. Yes, perhaps that was when I overcame a certain ambivalence, or stopped worrying about whether what I said about Judaism was right or wrong.

I believe that we must declare ourselves at critical junctures in our lives. For me, that declaration usually involves a headlong dive to reach dead center, my center, the place where the only voice I can hear is my own. It means creating my own answers and then, when they turn out to be wrong, creating them all over again.

The truth is, on the day I took tea with the rabbi I was nowhere near center. Truth is, when the rabbi leaned forward, I leaned back. When she asked what I'd gleaned, I balked. My brain froze.

"Go ahead," she said. "Tell me your wisdom."

Long pause.

"Lisa?"

"Can't say. I don't know right now." I shrugged. "I just don't."

145

• • •

The next day, at the Jewish Community Library, I got hold of an English translation of the Talmud. I chose one of the tractates at random, opened the pages, and began to read. It was then, my fingers following the digressions of rabbis throughout the ages, that I came to understand: I had something in common with these rabbis.

The gleanings. Why hadn't I realized it before? I too was creating mishnah. I too had gathered knowledge about Judaism piecemeal, from one person at a time, and had written down what I'd learned. Sure, the rabbis were leagues above me intellectually and knew more about Jewish law than I could ever hope to know. But we'd both followed a similar path. We'd questioned, listened, recorded, compiled.

The preceding spring I'd driven over a hundred miles to Elk, a tiny, wind-lashed coastal town up north, where the Navarro River serves as the mikvah. I'd talked with Ella Russell, the mikvah lady, in her kitchen while she chopped fresh carrots and peppers. She told me that she'd been leading women to the river for years. One by one she helped them down the muddy banks, heard them gasp as warm skin met cold water, hoped for their transformation. She blessed them when they couldn't bless themselves or stood silently in witness.

"We don't have a special building with a sunken bath," she said. "We've got the river, which is holy. It's living water." She stopped chopping, put down her knife. "You know what I find most beautiful? The moment during a mikvah when you get the sense, the most amazing sense, that you really are God."

Later I walked outdoors with the Elk rabbi, Margaret Holub, whose rural congregation had lacked a synagogue until recently. For years her congregants had carefully placed a Torah scroll in the back of a pickup, stuffed prayer shawls under their arms and prayerbooks under the seats, driven the dirt roads to a different house each Friday night and Saturday morning for worship. The rabbi and I ended up that morning in the middle of a May Day festival. Around us kids screamed their joy, wrapped rainbow ribbons around the long maypole. She told me that community was based in deeds, not in physical structures.

"The Talmud says these are the deeds whose reward is without measure: honoring your father and mother, burying the dead, taking care of the bride, taking care of the sick, welcoming guests, praying, studying. I often think of this as a checklist for what a community needs. A building, a synagogue—this was never the important thing, at least not for us."

These voices were part of my gleanings. And now, in front of me was the Talmud, in which rabbis were arguing. I tried to follow their logic, keep track of their digressions. Nothing about the Talmud was linear. It was a collage, built layer upon layer. It was a Website in book form.

I tracked a discussion about the *mezuzah*, a case containing a holy parchment that Jews were supposed to affix to their doorposts. Was that *all* doorposts? Should one affix a mezuzah to the doorpost of a stable? A woodshed? A storehouse? A bathhouse? The rabbis argued round and round, got into the specifics of doorway height, talked about the nature of a dwelling (about whether a cell—a place you inhabited against your own free will—would be considered a dwelling, would require a mezuzah; whether a synagogue was a dwelling; whether all rooms of a synagogue would require a mezuzah), detoured into the role of women, and ended up with the question, *But are the synagogues of the villages subject to leprosy?* Then, miraculously, the discussion wound up back where it began.

This—all of this—was a search for truth. It was chaos with an inner order. It was life, the rabbis said; it was spirit. It was religion.

For laypeople, the nonordained, religion has often been difficult to define. In the essay "Characteristics of Religion," English anthropologist Rodney Needham noted that no word common to the Indo-European languages could be translated as *religion*. Nor, he continued, did any Greek or Latin word correspond exactly to the English word. He said the Latin etymology of "religion" was disputable and was able only to trace the word from *ligare*, to tie, or else from *leger*, to collect.

After reading the essay, I wondered about these words. Collect. Tie. Didn't they describe the Talmud? Each page was a collection of associative thoughts tied together, sometimes by the thinnest of threads. Perhaps *ligare* and *leger* were the right words after all. Religion, then, was a process of collecting shards of knowledge and tying them together. Collecting and tying, acts to be performed again and again in one's lifetime. In my lifetime.

That night I had a dream. The setting was a dark, cavernous room, and I stood at its center. Around me were hundreds of white votive candles. Somehow, I understood that I was to light each one. I did this without question. I lit a candle, and then another, slowly, methodically, moving on my knees from one to the next, watching as each flame came to life and reached upward. In the morning, when I awakened, I remembered the dream clearly. But what did it mean? Was I in the process of illuminating my own darkness?

Later that day I taped a small piece of paper, a quote from William James, to my computer. *We believe all that we can and would believe everything if we only could.*

David gave me a gift. It was the morning of our seventh wedding anniversary, two weeks after we'd become owners of a large mortgage and a used house. Earlier that morning, the latch to our new front gate had fallen off in my hand. The central heating had failed. Then the water pressure had mysteriously died while I stood, soaped up and baffled, staring at the showerhead. This was our home.

I was in my office, staring out the window, when David crept up from behind, wrapped his arms around me, kissed my neck. He turned to me, placed a long thin box in my hands.

"Happy anniversary, babe," he said. He waited expectantly.

I turned it over, raised it to eye level. "Concert tickets? Nose ring?"

"Nope. Neither."

I tipped the box ever so slightly. My gift-receiving skills had never been well honed. "Can I shake it?"

"You can open it, for starters."

I tore off the wrapping paper, lifted the top. I looked down. What I saw made my breath catch in my throat. I lifted the slender sculpted piece by its tip.

David shifted back and forth on his feet. "It's a mezuzah."

"I know." I'd never touched one before. I had, however, recently experienced a virtual mezuzah at a Website for mezuzah enthusiasts. (*Buy the Kinetic Star of David Mezuzah! Position and reposition any one of the six points of the Star of David yourself! Kosher parchment scroll included!*)

The word *mezuzah*, the site had explained, was Hebrew for "doorpost." A small parchment scroll inscribed with two passages from the Torah was rolled up inside each mezuzah. The first part of the passages, the Shema, the central prayer of Judaism, was a call to God. The second part—according to my read—was a call to serve God.

I wracked my brain. Did I know anyone with a mezuzah? My parents had never had one. My mother's brother, my father's sister, my own brother and sister, my cousins and nephews and niece—no. Not a one. We were a family free of them. And my friends? I counted them off in my head. They came to zero, on the mezuzah score.

"Surprise," said David.

I turned it around in my hands. I held it up to the light. I put it down on the desk. I looked at David.

David ran his finger down the sides, up the center of the mezuzah, watching me intently. I hadn't said a word. He stepped closer, put his lips near my ear. "Anyone home?" he said softly.

"It's beautiful," I said. And it was. The artist had melded together two different kinds of metal. Whorls of copper attached themselves like wings to a small tube of bronze-colored aluminum. I looked at David. I wanted to tell him. I couldn't tell him. The mezuzah wasn't going on our front door.

I wasn't ready to declare myself. And I wasn't sure what hanging the mezuzah would mean. Did the mezuzah represent who I was or even where I was with my Judaism? Did it represent David? Could it? And what about other people, people who came to visit—what would they think? Most of my neighbors weren't Jewish. Did I want them to think, *She's a Jew*, as they crossed my threshold? What about the Jews I knew? Did I want them to think, *She's a religious Jew*, as they stepped into my house?

"Ready?" said David.

"For what?"

"To affix the mezuzah." He made a ceremonious bow toward me. I stared at him blankly.

He straightened, made a move toward my hand. "The front door. Let's put it up."

My fingers tightened around the metal. "No—I mean, not now."

"Later?"

"No. I . . . I don't want it on the door."

He rubbed his forehead. "Why not?"

"I just don't." I shrugged.

"But it's an act of faith."

"No. It's an act of identity."

"So *what?*"

I looked down, opened my palm, inspected the mezuzah more closely. I uncorked the central tube and peered in. Nothing. Where was the prayer? I looked up at David.

I swallowed hard. "Something's not here."

He brightened. "Right. We can create our own blessing. I thought we'd write it together, roll it up, slip it in." He scanned the books on the shelf. "Or, if you want, we can choose a poem we love. Neruda,

Mary Oliver—maybe even one of Rumi's. We can put the words we choose at the threshold of our door."

I struggled with my thoughts. Why would we create our own mezuzah scroll? It seemed contrived, like celebrating Christmas in L.A. You needed snow, real pine, cold hands.

"I don't think that'll work for me," I said softly.

I stood there. Then carefully, as though moving glass or flowers—things you could break or kill—I put the mezuzah back in its box, leaving off the lid. Morning light filtered through the drapes. I set the box upright on my desk, making the whole length of the mezuzah visible. It was a wondrous gift in many ways. Why wasn't I thrilled?

I wanted to feel the way I had when I woke one morning to find that David had scattered red rose petals—hundreds of them—everywhere. I saw them, piled in little hills on my nightstand, lying like great folds of velvet on the blanket. I felt them, like soft red lips on my chest. I even found some in my hair.

That was David. His gestures were unusual. They affirmed life. And now, this. It was a demarcation of some sort. A declaration.

Our silence was polite and confused.

"Maybe we should talk about this another time," said David.

I nodded. I forced a smile. I said what I should: "Thanks for the gift."

What do you do with an off-the-door mezuzah? Do you keep it in the box? Do you take it out, stand it up, rest it against the windowpane? Or do you carry it outside, plant it near the bird of paradise? Do you stare at it fearfully, day after day, wondering whether prolonged mezuzah mistreatment will mean that the rest of your life is entirely screwed? Do you wake up one day, wondering how the mezuzah ended up on the refrigerator door?

"What's up?" yelled my friend Mindy Bernstein over the phone. "I'm at the warehouse, so I can't talk long," she shrieked. Her business,

Cold Fish, made refrigerator magnets, the fancy kind, for a living. Pottery Barn loved them. They sold out at Starbucks, stunned the buyers at Crate and Barrel.

"I'm staring at the fridge," I said.

"What?"

"There's a mezuzah on my refrigerator door."

"You got rid of my magnets?" she shrieked.

"No. Relax. The Fall '99 collection is holding up the mezuzah. The hip orange ladybugs."

"They were Spring '98, actually. You bought a mezuzah?" I heard the sound of an adding machine in the background. "Sorry," she said over the noise, "I have to multitask. So what's with the mezuzah?"

"David bought it."

"Oh?" Thwack. Crack. Total amount.

"Mindy," I said, raising my voice to compete. "It was my anniversary gift. You think I should put it on the front door?"

"It's a better spot than the fridge."

"Very funny. I'm feeling a little weird about the whole idea. Plus, there's no prayer inside."

"No prayer? What *is* inside?"

"It's empty. David wants us to create our own blessing."

"You can't do that. It's a mezuzah. It's like, a set thing. There's a history, a tradition. It's not a Christmas tree ornament." Silence. "God," she said under her breath, "I could do tree ornaments. They'd be in the market by the holidays."

"Mindy? Hello? Are you with me?"

"Yes. Of course. Look, babycakes. This is what I think. You have to use the Jewish prayer. What else can you do? You want to write your own—what? A little ditty? You want to put a little ditty in something as old as a mezuzah? If you're going to do something traditional, then be traditional. If you want to write your own thing, fine; write it and just tape it up to the door. But don't put it in the mezuzah. It's not part of the package."

"Do you have a mezuzah?" I said.

"No! Are you nuts? I'm not that kind of Jew! I'm not religious at all." Mindy paused. Someone was shouting in the background. "Hold on, sweetheart—Dino? You all right? What? Dino? I'll be right there. Lisa, sweetheart—gotta go. Kisses."

I took the mezuzah from the fridge. I kept it near me, in my office, and began to examine it more closely each day. Someone, an artist, had created it by hand, and the result was magnificent, with few irregularities.

I found out through a pamphlet called *Like a Reed: The Message of the Mezuza* that the passages placed inside the mezuzah were supposed to be inscribed by hand. A *sofer*, a Jewish scribe, wrote out each one, carefully concentrating on the meaning of the mezuzah as he wrote. A mezuzah printed by machine would lack intention. "Just as the sofer puts great thought and care into writing each mezuza," the pamphlet said, "so those who see the mezuza should think about all that it represents." The page had a photo of a scribe— of his hand, really—as it held the pen and wrote in small, careful print the passages that called out to God.

One night, when David and I were in bed, I said, "Can we talk about it?"

"It? Does *it* begin with M?"

"No. P."

David rubbed his eyes. "P?"

"Parchment."

He smiled. "Of course. And P is for pleasure."

"And persistence."

He laughed, stroked my cheek. "Go ahead."

"You sure you're up for this?"

"Mmm. Yeah." He leaned his head back on the pillow. "Talk to me."

I reached over, turned off the light. "I'd like us to put up the mezuzah, but I don't want to substitute something we've written ourselves for the prayer. I think we should put the traditional Torah portion in it."

Silence.

"David?"

"I'm here. I'm awake. Now tell me why."

I found myself staring out into the darkness. "I think it has something to do with the word difficult. Difficult isn't necessarily something I want to avoid anymore, when it comes to Judaism. The prayer is difficult for me. Difficult for me to relate to, difficult for me to put in historical perspective, and difficult for me to read, because I don't read Hebrew. Two years ago, these would've been reasons enough to trash the idea of using the prayer. Right? I would've headed straight for a poem."

I brushed my hand over David's forehead. "But now? That choice seems too easy, feels as if I'd be sidestepping something important. I'm in a relationship with that Torah passage, just like I'm in a relationship with Judaism. And I know that relationship will change with time. The way I read the passage today will be different from the way I read and understand it next year, or the year after, or even ten years from now. You know what I'm saying? Things unfold. And they keep unfolding."

I paused. I lowered my voice and spoke slowly. "But it's all very Jewish, isn't it? And where does that leave you? It's your house too; it's our house. Why did you buy the mezuzah? Was it a gift for me? A gift for us?"

No reply.

"David?"

He pressed his hand against mine. The room was so dark I couldn't see his eyes. "I'm connected to Judaism in two ways," he said. "One way is through you. I'm therefore connected to Judaism forever. The other way is through affinity. I've always had a cultural affinity—I wouldn't say it's a religious affinity—for Judaism. I've always been drawn to Jewish people, interested in Jewish history.

"I bought the mezuzah for you, and I bought it for us. For you because you're Jewish, and for us because it's our home. It's our home. So I'd like the mezuzah to mean something to both of us."

We lay there, stumped, for a few minutes.

An idea arose. "I know. What if we double up? What if we put the Torah passage in the mezuzah, along with a piece of writing of our choice?" I stopped to think. "Maybe the Marge Piercy poem, the one on my bulletin board upstairs. It begins beautifully: 'Connections are made slowly, sometimes they grow underground. You cannot always tell by looking at what is happening.'"

Silence. I began to see shapes in the darkness.

"David?"

"I'd like to use our wedding vows with the Torah passage."

Years ago, in a late-night session sometime before our wedding, we had carefully crafted our vows. Then we had asked a friend, an artist, to create something akin to a *ketuba*, a traditional Jewish wedding contract. The one she made for us was a collage of Japanese paper images with our vows superimposed. We signed it. Our families signed it. And then, mysteriously, the day after the wedding it disappeared. We never saw it again. Luckily, we had a copy of the vows.

I hugged him.

"Does that mean you like the idea?" he said.

"Mmm. Very much." I leaned my body into his, rested my head on his chest.

A beginning, an end, a beginning.

I play a game with the Talmud these days. It's a form of bibliomancy. I think of it as a Jewish version of tarot or I Ching. It goes like this: I ask the Talmud a question, one that can't be answered with a yes or a no. Then I open a tractate, a volume, at random and let my finger land on a passage. Any passage. No matter how obscure the text, I try to let it lead me, help me find an answer.

Recently, I asked the Talmud, "What kind of Jew will I become?"

I opened the book, watched my index finger crash-land in the middle of the page next to these words:

A favourite saying of Rab was: the future world is not like this world.

First, this world. The *New York Times* recently featured an article about a nationwide poll of young Roman Catholics. The poll, which measured something the pollsters were calling "essential Catholicism," found that the majority of young Catholics saw Catholicism as involving only a few core elements that were essential to the faith. You needed to believe that God was present in the sacraments, you needed a love for the Virgin Mary, and you needed to help the poor. The pope, priests, nuns, monks—they weren't, according to the majority, basic to the faith. The institutions of Catholicism were less important to the respondents than the essentials.

What was essential to Judaism? To my Judaism? Books and people. People and books. There were books that explained the Talmud and the Torah. There were books on Jewish history and culture, first-person accounts of the Holocaust, thick tomes on whether or not God was a verb, books that defined earth-based Judaism or asked why oranges sat on the seder plate; there were books that explored mysticism, mitzvot, practice, and prayer. And of course there was the Talmud itself, the Torah itself, books I believed would be more and more important to me as time went on.

People and books. It was October, the month of the Jewish new year, and outside my window wind was bending the branches of a eucalyptus. The newly converted Mark McCormick and I had decided just the week before that for the new year we'd read the Torah together. We'd walked to the Jewish bookstore, bought two different translations of the Torah, along with a calendar showing which portion was to be read each week.

Mark had taken on an additional name—the Hebrew name Chaim—upon converting. The word meant "life." And life, he said, was the affirmation he heard in his head when he thought of himself as a Jew.

Yes, people. Rabbis too. They were heart and brain, and they were human. Unlike priests, they made love, lived in the world of the flesh as well as the spirit. Rabbis were like walking bodies of knowledge. They were lines of continuity and demarcation. They were reflections of entire communities. They were teachers, and the best of them knew how to teach people to teach themselves.

The future world is not like this world. I knew this about myself: the Jew I was today differed from the Jew I'd be tomorrow. My Judaism was a trajectory, a continuum, an intuitive process punctuated by moments of cognition. Some days it was a brain-based religious thing, full of demands for logic and a grapple with text. Some days it was a feeling of identity. Some days it was in my body, my marrow; it coursed through my veins. Some days it was something best understood by the senses. On those days I often found a few seconds of peace, a sense of wholeness.

The future world is not like this world. I imagined the future. I imagined an urban, Bay Area, postmillennial Jewish scenario. I imagined the One-Tribe Card, a card you could buy at the beginning of the new year. The card meant that you had contributed money to the Jewish community (a nice thing to do) and entitled you to membership in and/or admittance to not one synagogue but all the synagogues in the Bay Area, plus the Jewish Museum, the Jewish Community Library, performances of the Traveling Jewish Theater, and the Jewish Film Festival. (Why? Because Judaism was manifested at places outside of temple as well; because the majority of American Jews did, after all, define themselves as Jews-by-culture.)

If you were already a one-synagogue-affiliated Jew, then most likely one particular synagogue would be your home base. But you'd feel free, entitled even, to visit other synagogues, whether Reform, Renewal, Orthodox, or Reconstructionist. You'd be exposed to other ways of worship, other people, different rabbis. You could drop in on a course about kabbalah at the Renewal synagogue or one about Judaism and social justice at the Reconstructionist place of worship (which would probably be a space shared with Unitarians). The lines of demarcation between Jews might begin to melt.

When was the last time the boundaries between Jews had disintegrated? When was the last time one branch of Judaism didn't define itself against another? Was it during the Holocaust? Was it in the camps, where people prayed together secretively, quietly, hungrily, behind barbed wire? Must we join together only in opposition to a force that wants our annihilation?

The future world is not like this world. Outside my window, the wind had calmed. In two weeks, Mark and I would begin reading the Torah. Tomorrow, David and I would hang the mezuzah.

What kind of Jew will I become? The kind of Jew I am becoming.

He dropped the nail. I heard the *clink!* as it hit the ground. The hole in the mezuzah was so small that it had taken us twenty minutes to find the right-sized nail, which was the thinness of a thread. Then, standing together in the doorway, with the dog underfoot and confused (are they going to take me for a walk?), David dropped the nail—not once but three times—as he tried to bang the mezuzah into the doorframe.

I thought I could do a better job, and told him so. Then, with the dog sniffing at my pocket and a siren blaring somewhere in the distance, I tried too, and dropped the nail. I glared at the dog, then yelled at him to go lie down. David looked at me reproachfully. And then I felt guilty for yelling at the dog at all—but especially during a holy moment, the moment when we were hanging our first mezuzah.

And so that was the way it went. It happened to be the eve of Rosh

Hashanah, the new year. The sun was lowering and it was important to both of us to hang the mezuzah before sunset.

Finally David banged it in.

The air began to cool. David unrolled the small piece of paper containing our vows. We had copied them by hand, each of us alternating, writing a few lines and handing back the pen. We read the words together, softly, so as not to alarm the neighbors. "I promise that I'll see who you are, that I'll see who you believe you are, that I'll talk when I have something to say, that I'll set things aright when they've fallen, that I'll walk beside you when you need company, that I'll kiss you when you're sad, that I'll hold you when you need comfort, that I'll get you lost when things become too familiar, that I'll find you when you're lost, that I'll argue when I think you're wrong, that I'll listen when you're talking, that I'll laugh when you laugh, that I'll cry when you cry, that I'll read what you write, that I'll see what is plain, that I'll listen to what is fair, that I'll taste what is bitter, that I'll smell what is sweet, that I'll touch what is soft, that I'll look for the truth, and that I'll always love you."

The sun set lower in the sky. The dog was once again at my feet. I patted his head. I opened the Torah to Deuteronomy, to the first passage of the mezuzah scroll. I read aloud the passage that would be on our doorway, that would greet me every time I crossed the threshold. "Listen Israel, the Lord is our God, the Lord is one. You shall love the Lord your God with all your heart, with all your soul, with all your strength. These words which I command you today shall be in your heart. You shall teach them to your children and speak about them when you sit at home, walk about, lie down, or get up. You shall tie them as a symbol on your arm and as a headpiece between your eyes. You shall write them on the doorways of your house and on your gates."

We were silent for a moment. The siren in the distance no longer shrieked. The freeway noise, which the realtor had compared to the roar of the ocean, was miraculously absent. We held hands, even though we were married, and had been for seven years. We looked at the mezuzah.

I felt a rush of some sort. It began in the center of my chest and spread outward. It was a kind of heat, something that deepened and then dissipated. Call it love. Call it God. Call it a physical epiphany. I'm not sure what exactly happened to me while we stood there, David and I, holding hands. But that night it seemed to me that Judaism was a quiet revelation. Sometimes, I thought, like noon on the Navarro River, or a half-moon against the black sky, it was a thing beautiful in silence.

EXILE

I'm in Boston, at a place called Rites of Passage, with my friend Lauren. We're topless, exposed to each other under a fluorescent light and about to be tattooed—painted, really, with a henna concoction—by a woman named Juliette. Every inch of Juliette's arms is tattooed. I see green dragons, blue-black birds with their wings spread, a woman's dark silhouette, a dagger dripping blood, a red heart. She stares at us critically, an artist with one eye half-shut, a paintbrush in one hand, a palmful of wet henna powder in the other.

"What'll it be?" she asks.

"Maybe a vine, a beautiful one that starts here and moves upward," Lauren says. Her index finger circles around her navel, then travels snakelike up her stomach, between and around her breasts. "Paint flowers and leaves too," she says. "Cover me, in fact." She takes a breath and exhales. "I'm getting married tomorrow. I'll be naked for the ceremony. It's a pagan thing."

"Cool," says Juliette, unfazed. She surveys Lauren's flesh.

"I'm not a pagan, though," says Lauren.

Juliette looks up, shrugs. "Whatever."

Lauren looks at me. The room is cold. An antique gynecological exam table holds center stage. We're uncomfortable, a bit awkward even, facing each other without our shirts. I shift back and forth on my feet. Lauren stares at the table, then at the ceiling. Juliette leans over, aims her brush at Lauren's stomach, and begins painting. As she works, the tip of her tongue escapes from between her lips.

Lauren is getting married to a man who isn't Jewish. They'll marry twice: once in the morning, in a naked ceremony headed by two witches, and once in the evening, at the civilized home of her aunt. I'm to be a best woman of sorts in the pagan gig. This means I'll have to drop my clothes and step round Lauren's living room clockwise, sprinkling water into the air with wide gestures, while another nude victim—I mean friend—of Lauren's burns a thick smudge-stick of sage and waves it at invisible spirits.

Lauren had originally assumed she'd be married by a rabbi. The rabbis she and Kyle met with when they were planning their wedding had asked for assurance that their children, who didn't yet exist, who may never exist, would be raised Jewish. One rabbi leaned forward in his chair, placed his palms on his desk, looked at Lauren, and said, "You know this is important, right?"

Lauren shrugged her shoulders. Kyle let his eyes wander around the room. After meeting with the fourth rabbi in four weeks, Kyle went home, called the witches.

"Sure," they said. "We'll do it. We'll marry the two of you."

During the past year, Lauren has met with a priest once a week. She sought him out, she told me, because Judaism is a religion of rules, of gnarled old men. It's a dry landscape, a desert, a place where nothing can grow. Christianity, on the other hand, is about love, not discipline, she said. It's about heart, not will. It's an oasis—verdant, lush. For awhile, I thought she might leave the tribe, become an exile from Judaism. The idea sent small waves of panic through me. We shared a heritage, even if it was one we were unsure about how to manifest in our daily lives. We had a connection.

Juliette is gently painting Lauren's skin and ends with a belt of tear-shaped leaves around her waist. Then Juliette leans over, reaches for a fan in the corner, turns it toward Lauren, and hits the high-speed button.

"That's so the paint will dry," she says by way of explanation. I watch goosebumps rise on Lauren's arms.

Juliette turns to me. "Let's hear it," she says. "Describe what you want." Her sketch pad is poised.

"A vine that wends," I say. My finger glides up my stomach, between my breasts, up and over my right shoulder. "That's the trail."

"Mmm. A flower would be nice too," says Juliette, hunched over her pad. "I mean at the end of the vine, on the back of your shoulder." She turns and shows me the drawing.

No, I think. An idea comes to me with surprising strength. "I want a star of David."

Juliette raises an eyebrow. Lauren opens her mouth and closes it again. The fan is making her hair wave wildly.

I was sure of it. I wanted this. A sign on my body. A star on my skin. Jew. Juif. Juden. Lauren looks amused, then a flash of—was it pride?—lights her face.

Juliette quickly bends over her pad. Her pencil moves rapidly. "Here," she says, showing me the sketch. "Is this what you want?"

I look at her rendering. A six-pointed star hangs off a vine. Leaves fall in and out of the center. It looks like something Eve might have worn in the garden. It's perfect. I nod my head.

As the wet brush flattens against my skin, I close my eyes. Lauren air-dries next to me. She and Juliette begin to talk about bodies. "I can't stand my breasts," Lauren says. "They're way too big."

I've heard this before. She means it. "Your breasts," I say, opening my eyes, "are fine. They're beautiful."

There's a way in which we despise the essential elements of ourselves. Our breasts, our hair, our nose, our face, our voice, our heart. Our thoughts. Our race. Our religion. They become our enemies. It happens quietly. It happens in tattoo parlors and churches, in synagogues and schools. It happens in small pink rooms on suburban streets. It happens in our mind. We learn to be in exile from our body, from our spirit, from our self. We turn away from who we are.

Jews are experts at exile. At first it was a geographical thing. A creased photocopy of an ancient map of Europe on my bulletin board tells part of the story. At the top, in uneven script, it says, *Expulsions, Middle Ages: Jews.* In the bottom corner it says neatly, *Direction of the flight and dispersal of expelled Jews.* Then there are arrows. They point everywhere. The entire page is filled with the black swirls of arrows curving their way into and out of continents.

Sometimes entire regions or countries forced Jews out, and in many cases not once but again and again. These European places boasted of major expulsions: England, France, Hungary, Austria, Bavaria, Silesia, Spain, Sardinia, Lithuania, Bohemia, Moravia, Saxony, Sicily, Malta, Crimea. Poland was nice for awhile but then turned nasty. Towns and cities too—the map was littered: Breslau, Tlemcen, Strasbourg, Naples, Palermo, Bergamo, Cracow, Geneva, Lucerne, Bern.

Most of Jewish history—more than three thousand years—is characterized by geographical expulsions. Morris Grossman, in an essay called "Exiled from Exile," writes that for modern Jews, exile has become part of our collective mentality. Exile is our ongoing internal state of being. He's not talking about geographic exile here. He's not talking about exile from a historical, biblical homeland. He's talking about personal, psychological, and metaphysical exile. "To be in exile," he says, "is to have a mission and purpose in life." The mission is about returning to one's roots, one's authentic nature, one's proper place of being.

In 1948, Israel was established as a Jewish state. This meant that suddenly all Jews living outside of Israel were categorized as diaspora Jews. Technically, Jews now have a homeland, a place from which many of us are in exile. Jews are experts at exile. Even the Dalai Lama wants to know how we do it, how we live so far away from our homeland yet remain a people.

Every week when I do tai chi at an elementary school near my home, my path crosses that of a young African-American man. He usually wears a pendant in the shape of Africa around his neck. Sometimes he wears a scarf made of kente cloth. For about a year we simply nodded to each other; then we tentatively began saying hello. Now we talk. I know he's a teacher at the school. Recently, I asked to see his pendant. He leaned his shoulders toward me, allowing Africa to dangle.

I fingered it. I looked up. I asked the question that had been at the back of my mind for months. "Why do you wear it?"

He looked incredulous. "It's the mother country," he said, "the homeland. Don't you get it?"

I didn't. The notion of homeland for me meant the land in which I lived. I don't wear a pendant in the shape of Israel. *Next year in Jerusalem* isn't my mantra. Perhaps, like so many American Jews of my generation, I simply don't consider myself in exile from Israel. Perhaps I lack a sense of Jewish loyalty, or of nostalgia. Perhaps I know that unity with the motherland is one of life's perpetually unfulfilled dreams, a kind of archetypal yearning.

We're at an astounding time in Jewish history: no country is exiling Jews. Except Israel. But Jews are experts at exile. So now we're in exile from our nature, or in exile from each other. Many ultra-Orthodox scowl at the rest of us. They push us out, perceive us as aberrations.

Juliette is behind me now. Her brush moves like water down my back. "There," she says. "Finished. Have a look."

I step to the full-length mirror. A vine makes its way over the landscape of my body. Lauren moves next to me and suddenly we're facing our images. We're two Jews, topless, exposed, with goosebumps and tattooed lines on our flesh. The lines curve and dip, demarcating our continents: breasts, ribs, stomach, hips. I think back to the map on my wall at home, to the arrows of Jewish exile.

We're maps, both of us. The lines of exile have crisscrossed our bodies, entered our blood, inhabited our minds.

I twist my body so that in the mirror I can see the star of David on my back. Lauren turns, peers at it. She leans over, traces its outline with her finger. She steps back, looks directly at me. "A Jewess," she says, nodding her head. "A definite Jewess."

The mirror is an affirmation: I look Jewish. Right now, I look very Jewish. I may even look too Jewish. I want this. Tomorrow I'll wear the star of David on my naked back in front of strangers at a pagan wedding. For the next three weeks—until the henna wears off—I'll wear shirts that expose the back of my shoulder, the star, everywhere I go.

"Jew," I say to myself.

Somehow, I've learned the thing that matters. In the years that have passed since I began my journey into Judaism, I've changed. I've become Jewish by choice as much as by birth.

What do I know about my own Judaism? The question begs others. Can something be fluid and fixed at the same time? Can something be beautiful and invisible, difficult and full of grace? Can it live in the heart as well as the mind?

I touch the line between my breasts, follow it down. Vine. Flesh. Vine. Flesh. There is the vine. There is me. There's Judaism, the religion of paradox and reconciliation. I'll learn from it what I can. I'll sort out my own conflicted truths. I refuse to reject myself—any part. I no longer choose exile.

Juliette and Lauren are looking at me, as if waiting. I stretch an arm over my shoulder, guide my fingers to the damp star on my back. I want to tell Lauren what I know. I want to tell her, *This star will not fade.* I know this. I'll feel it always, in my fingers, in my flesh.

CPSIA information can be obtained
at www.ICGtesting.com
Printed in the USA
LVOW13s1238230718
584638LV00006B/18/P